Psychotherapy
and a
Christian View of Man

By

DAVID E. ROBERTS

D1572390

NEW YORK

CHARLES SCRIBNER'S SONS

To

ELLIE

PREFACE

IN THIS BOOK I use "psychiatry," "psychotherapy" and "psycho-analysis" more or less interchangeably because, in view of the non-technical character of the chapters on psychology, no useful purpose would be served in making the necessary distinctions. Strictly speaking, however, "psychiatry" involves the whole range of medical care for the mentally ill. "Psychotherapy" is one specific technique within that range. And if the wishes of Freudians were followed, "psycho-analysis" would be used only in connection with their form of psychotherapy. It would be cumbersome, however, to use a different word or phrase whenever a departure from Freudianism is involved, even though both Jung and Adler have taken the trouble to furnish distinctive labels for their theories. Instead, I have simply called attention to modifications of Freud's doctrines, or disagreements with them, at relevant points in the text. Psychiatrists must possess the M.D. degree; but not all psychotherapists or psycho-analysts are M.D.s, and not all psychiatrists are psycho-analytically oriented.

I should like to express gratitude to several individuals and groups without in any way implicating them in responsibility for what I have written. I have profited greatly from extended conversations with Harry Bone, Ph.D. (Consulting Psychologist), Hiram K. Johnson, M.D. (Psychiatrist at the Rockland State Hospital), and Paul Tillich, Ph.D., D.D. (now University Pro-

fessor at Harvard University, Cambridge, Massachusetts).
Professor John C. Bennett, also of Union Seminary, and two
psychiatrists—Drs. Harry M. Tiebout and Sol Ginsberg—very
kindly read a first draft of the whole manuscript, as did Professor
Tillich. I am indebted also, in various ways, to the members of
the seminar on "Religion and Health" at Columbia University,
especially to its Chairman, Professor Horace L. Friess; to the
Council for the Clinical Training of Theological Students; and
to the Commission on Religion and Health of the Federal Council of Churches. At Union Theological Seminary I am grateful to colleagues and students generally for comradeship and
criticism, especially to those students who have participated with
Dr. Johnson and myself in a course on "Theology and Psychiatry." Finally, although a preface is not the place to try to use
language adequate to express the fact, I have been helped in
writing this book, as in all things, by my wife, Elinor, and our
daughter, Kathleen.

D. E. R.

Contents

CONTENTS

PSYCHOTHERAPY
AND A
CHRISTIAN VIEW OF MAN

INTRODUCTION

THIS BOOK REVOLVES around two main foci. Psychotherapy
and Christian theology are different disciplines,—one might even
say "radically" different. Each has a theoretical and a practical
side, and each will continue to carry on its work in accordance
with the concepts and methods that seem necessary or appropriate to those engaged in the respective tasks. But it is not enough
to declare that each should be left free in its own sphere, and
should be reminded of its limits when it encroaches illegitimately
upon other spheres. In the end nothing of human concern can
be excluded from the purview of either, and devotees of each
approach to "the whole" of human life are likely to regard the
one they follow as best suited to constitute a final court of appeal.
If one suggests that philosophy is in a position to decide wherein
either approach is legitimate or illegitimate, two embarrassments
arise. First, the judge (philosophy) is left sitting in an empty
court room because the contesting parties refuse to accept his
authority. The psychologist can show that all philosophical thinking is conditioned by the forces he describes. The theologian can
show that philosophical conclusions are conditioned by the presence or absence of religious faith. Secondly, it is extremely difficult in the twentieth century to identify the judge himself. If
one is to assign such decisive functions to philosophy, one must
be able to answer the question: "Whose philosophy?" And that
is the beginning of a battle, not the end of one.

Instead of starting with an attempt to adjudicate claims and
to arrange for a division of labor, this book begins at the point
where psychotherapy and Christian theology overlap, intertwine
and conflict. The confusion of the present situation is symbolized

by the fact that the word "anthropology," which stands for the study of man, has at least two distinct meanings. The first is "secular," the second theological. In the former case the term has been expanded so that it no longer refers exclusively to the study of primitive man; eventually it may be used quite properly to refer to a single science which embraces all aspects of psychology and sociology. In the latter case the term refers to a Christian doctrine, based upon Biblical views of man's origin, sin, freedom and destiny, which must be understood in the light of its integral relationship with other central Christian doctrines concerning God, Christ, the Church and the Kingdom of God.

Some exponents of each of these "anthropologies" never get a clear glimpse of the other. Instead of meeting on the same ground, they fire arguments back and forth from behind fortifications well established in advance. Yet these fortifications are not so much consciously prepared defenses as they are a structure of mental habits, methods, categories and assumptions erected in the normal course of carrying out a specific task. As a consequence, books which deliberately attempt to provide common ground for a discussion between psychotherapy and Christian theology are relatively rare. The references to psycho-analysis which one finds in the *works of theologians* are frequently abstract, second-hand, polemical and out of date. Many of the standard *volumes on the psychology of religion* do not devote special attention to either of the fields just mentioned. On the one side, psychotherapeutic contributions tend to become swallowed up in a general treatment of conflicting schools and tendencies in contemporary psychology. On the other side, these same volumes usually regard theological problems in the strict sense as falling outside their scope. The *writings of psychotherapists and psychiatrists* themselves ordinarily deal with religious belief solely as a "cultural phenomenon," if they deal with it at all, and they do not take account of what have become in recent years the chief issues in Protestant theology. Finally, *books on pastoral psychology and counseling* are intended primarily to help the minister understand emotional problems, instead of to clarify his doctrinal thinking.

There are notable exceptions to these remarks, and I am deeply indebted to workers in each field who have seriously sought to understand the other. In personal experience with both psychotherapists and theologians I have found that the chief obstacle is the provincialism which attends expertness. Being human, they behave somewhat like families. Inside the group there are many quarrels between individuals and factions; it is only when the group is attacked from outside that one realizes how "closed" it is. The stock refutation of the outsider, in each case, is that "he doesn't really know much at first hand" about the position of the insider. Expertness lends plausibility to the refutation; but the difficulties which it raises in connection with communication are hard to exaggerate. Consequently it is almost impossible to find language about psychotherapy which a theologian can "understand," and *vice versa,* let alone to find language which is intelligible to one who is a layman in both fields. This book is intended, insofar as possible, to reach all three groups of readers, but with the foreknowledge that the expert will feel that less than justice has been done to his own subject.

A reader has the right to know at the outset where the author stands. Strictly speaking, however, that would mean beginning with a systematic discussion of the relations between psychotherapy and theology. Instead I have reserved treatment of this problem for the end of the book. Such a discussion is bound to be a bit difficult for some readers; and unless there is a foundation to build on, it is likely to be the least interesting. More important, however, is my concern to avoid the kind of initial "jockeying for position" which has vitiated much work on our problem. In the end one cannot escape the responsibility of taking a positive position; it will fall primarily within the framework of a psychotherapeutic or a theological orientation; or it will succeed in reaching a synthesis. Actually this book is an attempt to move in the direction of a synthesis. Initially, however, it is quite possible to begin inductively, examining psychotherapy and Christian theology as they are at the present moment. Indeed, any theoretical discussion of their ideal relationships is bound to be abstract and likely to be question-begging unless it takes into account what such a point of departure can disclose.

Therefore the plan of this book can be outlined as follows: Chapter I concentrates upon the practical considerations which make collaboration between Christianity and psychotherapy both desirable and difficult. Chapters II and III are an attempt to call attention to aspects of psychotherapy which are bound to be of interest to a Christian. These chapters describe the needs which psychotherapy seeks to meet and how it goes about meeting them. At this point one confronts a difficult decision. Either he must seek to expound the history and leading concepts of each of the groups that have made major contributions to psychiatry and psychotherapy, or he must try to fix upon some of the features that are more or less common property for all groups. Despite the fact that the latter alternative involves tearing concepts out of their context, I have adopted it. My main purpose in these two chapters is to convey to some one who knows little or nothing about psychotherapy an impression of how it obtains results that in some respects parallel what religion seeks to do. Consequently I keep the discussion at a level that the psychiatrist will rightly regard as elementary. Chapter IV establishes a link between the earlier and the latter part of the book. Granting that in the course of their practical work psychotherapists have made certain discoveries or rediscoveries about human motivation and character, what implications do these facts have for religious belief and training, and what light do they throw upon the relationship between faith and reason? The subsequent chapters deal with specific aspects of the Christian doctrine of man. They do not purport to cover, even sketchily, Christian doctrine as a whole. In principle, of course, such an inquiry could be pursued in connection with the teachings of any religion; but, in an effort to achieve some sharpness of focus, I have confined attention to issues which are at present the subject of lively debate in Protestantism. Here again, one is compelled to lift the relevant doctrinal concepts out of their context without going deeply into the circumstances which have set various types of Protestant thought in contrast or conflict with each other. The last chapter seeks to indicate lines along which a *rapprochement* between psychotherapy and Christian theology can be carried further.

CHAPTER I

Co-operation between Religion
and Psychotherapy

THE EFFECTS OF the initial hostility with which religious thinkers greeted Freud and the effects, in turn, of his remarks about religion, have not completely disappeared by any means. Nevertheless, within both psychiatric and Christian groups there are some who have found a harmonization between religious faith and mental health not only possible, but well-nigh inescapable. If further progress along these lines is to be made, it will come from those who are willing to lay aside rigid preconceptions in an effort to understand attitudes which may at first sight seem uncongenial to them. Collaboration cuts both ways. It can be blocked by religious thinkers who seize upon popular misrepresentations of psycho-analysis as an excuse for dismissing it without adequate examination. It can also be blocked by psychiatrists and psycho-analysts who hang onto formulæ for explaining away all religious belief as illusory, without testing and re-examining their formulæ in the light of a wide, sympathetic, first-hand acquaintance with religion at its best.

It is folly to deal with any great movement in human thought by fixing attention upon its most dubious aspects and then generalizing. Yet ignorance and ill-will still creep into many discussions of our topic. Often the criticisms of churchmen against psycho-analysis would be justified if what they describe really were the heart of psychotherapy. But invariably they are either based on second-hand information, the critic himself never having been directly exposed to psycho-analytic counseling; or they reflect the undeniable fact that such counseling can fail. There are many bunglers and charlatans who call themselves psycho-analysts; and there are types of cases where even the most skillful and fully trained doctors cannot obtain gratifying results. But no one would think of trying to discredit ordinary medical practice on the latter score; and only cranks would try to discredit it on the ground that there are incompetent doctors. Therefore probably the one salutary lesson to be learned from irresponsible attacks upon psychotherapy is that it does need uniform standards of licensure in order to weed out quacks.

Similar considerations need to be urged from the other side, however. Few psychiatrists are active Church members, and most of them are continually exposed only to those versions of religion which they encounter in their mentally ill patients. In reading the remarks of psychiatrists who are antagonistic to religion one sometimes encounters more or less penetrating criticisms of the Church and its beliefs; but the argument stops there. The writer thinks that he has succeeded in showing that "religion" or "Christianity" is neurotic, infantile and superfluous. The conclusion, of course, does not follow, any more than it follows that the "failures" of psycho-analysis give an adequate conception of its resources. Indeed, it is only when the discussion moves out of an atmosphere of argumentative debate and into an atmosphere of mutual search that real collaboration can begin.

This book is based upon the conviction that such collaboration is not only possible, but urgently needed. It is already going on in encouraging ways. Several joint conferences of pastors and psychiatrists have been held. Experiences in the chaplaincy during the war awakened many ministers to the desirability of cooperation with psychiatrists—and to their own lack of training in pastoral counseling. An increasing number of churches are adding psychiatrists to their regular staffs. Through clinical training and through courses in counseling, theological seminaries are extending the facilities whereby pastors may acquire greater knowledge and competence in helping people who suffer from emotional conflicts. Indeed, a significant proportion of the clergy now have a favorable, even an eager, attitude toward obtaining whatever enlightenment and assistance they can from psychotherapy. This attitude has already had considerable influence, in turn, upon lay members of the Church, and it will continue to have an increasing effect in the years that lie ahead. One of the most baffling aspects of the problem of mental health in America is, of course, the shortage of adequately trained people. There are not enough psychiatrists to staff our mental hospitals, at a time when public opinion is clamoring for expansion and improvement of such facilities. Outside large cities it is extremely difficult to get expert help for neurotic patients and even when such help is accessible it is beyond the pocket-books of many who need it. All of these considerations indicate that the psychiatric profession cannot be expected to cope with the problem by itself. It needs maximum help from schools, courts, social-service agencies, and from every other institution or profession that deals with people in their family relationships and their personal troubles. The Church and its ministers are much more aware of the problem and much more willing to co-operate in meeting it than was the case a generation ago. Often the minister is the only person in the community, outside members of the immediate family, to whom people confide their troubles. Moreover, a skillfully guided church congregation can do much, by its attitude, to provide acceptance and encouragement to a needy individual.

Therefore the Church should be looked upon by the psychiatric profession as a potential ally of enormous importance. It can do much, through a properly trained clergy, to remove the prejudices which often prevent mental illness from being diagnosed and treated as early as possible. The pastor himself—again, if properly trained—can deal with many pressing personal problems which will never reach a psychiatrist's office. Whether he is properly trained or not, he will perforce be dealing with emotional problems all the time, and what he does, for better or for worse, may be the only thing that is accomplished apart from the help or hindrance offered by friends and family.

The most important respect in which psychiatry can look to the clergy and other professions concerns the *preventive* side. In the process of dealing with seriously sick people, medical psychology has discovered certain principles which have a wide applicability to all human beings. At present there is great need for "educating" those who deal with human problems in such a way that they can use these principles effectively. The "educating" involves not merely learning some information that can be gleaned from a book on psychology; it involves self-understanding on the part of the person who wants to be in a position to offer help; and in many instances it involves a profound alteration of his own motives and attitudes. Because the Church plays an important role in shaping the moral assumptions of a community, it is bound to exercise a steady influence *either in the prevention or in the aggravation* of mental illness. Part of its task, in learning increasingly how to exert a beneficent instead of a harmful influence, involves examining its own beliefs and practices in the light of what psychotherapy has to offer. But it cannot do this unless principles of mental health are made available in a way that is relevant to the specific situation in which a minister or any other religious believer finds himself.

This last remark suggests one of the points at which some co-operation has already occurred, but where there is much room for further developments. In general, there has not yet arisen within the ranks of psychiatry an adequate understanding of the religious situation of our age. This is not surprising. It is almost impossible for a contemporary man to be expert in more than one field. The processes by which he masters one profession tend to shut him off from being able to understand the special responsibilities and perspectives of another. There are additional considerations which may make it difficult for a psychiatrist to take a sympathetic interest in Christianity. He may feel that all attempts to understand the problems of human life by other than scientific means are not only superfluous, but intellectually disreputable. He may have first-hand acquaintance with attitudes on the part of ministers and other religious people which have played an important role in causing the conflicts and confusions he has found in his patients. He may, with considerable justification, believe that organized religion goes hand in hand with forces in our culture which prevent human beings from reaching full emotional maturity. Or at least he may have decided that religion does very little effectively to counteract these harmful forces.

In commenting upon these unfavorable attitudes toward religion we might well draw an analogy between the Church and the growth of an individual. The analogy is not exact because institutions usually cannot be transformed dramatically and, so to speak, overnight, as individuals sometimes can be; yet even concerning this point it is well to recall that the Church has undergone significant and startling reformations. Suffice it to say, however, that no individual can be helped merely by attacking and, if possible, destroying what he takes to be the very basis of his life—his essential purposes, the foundation of his security, his most precious ideals and convictions. Even if one can convince him rationally that his beliefs are untenable, he is not likely to be helped by negative criticism. A really "therapeutic" procedure involves enabling him to discover and bring to expression whatever resources of strength and creativeness lie within him; once he has developed a realistic confidence in his own capacity to cope with life, the defensive attitude which he formerly employed in hanging onto his old illusions and mistakes will disappear. When we apply this analogy to the Church (without intending to suggest that it is like a sick patient!), it discloses the fruitlessness of listing the Church's defects, dismissing its beliefs as ridiculous, and then scolding it for failing promptly to "see the light," bow itself out of existence, and gladly admit that psychotherapy has all the answers. Yet some psychiatrists adopt attitudes toward Christianity which go directly counter, in such ways as the foregoing, to their own knowledge of human dynamics.

Finally, because they are specialists, they may fail to appreciate how forbidding and confusing their subject is to nonspecialists. Picture the predicament of a religious person who is willing to examine his beliefs in the light of what psychotherapy has to say. Assume that if he finds adequate reasons for altering his beliefs, he will do so. The more he investigates "what psychotherapy says," the more he discovers that the word covers a multitude of schools, factions and tendencies as bewildering as Protestantism itself! In his ignorance he does not want to make snap judgments; yet in order to become well enough informed to make a dependable judgment he must familiarize himself with a literature and a jargon that at first may seem weird, complicated and even repulsive. After having learned what he could, by the same methods he uses in studying anything else, he may be told (as we have already suggested) that his knowledge is more or less worthless because he has not been analyzed himself.

The various sources of misunderstanding which we have examined make it doubly desirable that both religious and psychiatric groups shall continue to work at the task of learning how to put aside prejudices which prevent a fruitful examination of each other's resources. The genius and the devotion to human betterment which have gone into both the Christian tradition and the development of medical psychology are far too imposing to be dismissed with a single *caveat*. And neither Christian belief nor psychiatric thinking has reached such perfect clarity and effectiveness that further attempts to evaluate either one are superfluous.

There is a special reason, not yet mentioned, why they should form an alliance in the present situation. The causes of panic, hopelessness and hostility are not only widespread and deeply rooted in our society; the price of failure to remove them is sure disaster. The political decisions and social movements which will determine the future, insofar as it can be affected by human intention at all, will reflect the *internal* condition, the character-structure, of contemporary men and women. No attempt to change ourselves internally can be divorced from a consideration of those economic, political and social conditions that so crucially affect the sort of individuals we become. Yet it is misleading to believe that even the most astute policies in social planning, government or diplomacy can be carried through unless such psychological factors as anxiety, hatred and will-to-power are taken into account. Fortunately we do not have to choose between external and internal remedies. Nor do we have to assert that civilization will be saved, if it is saved, by a single means

—whether it be economic, political, psychological or religious. But it is worth acknowledging that one of the most ominous features of contemporary life is the feeling of fatalism on the part of the individual. He tends to assume that his future lies wholly in the hands of forces which he cannot direct at all, or can influence only to an insignificant degree. This assumption reflects another one, namely, that what determines his security or insecurity, his success or failure, the worth or futility of his life, is something outside himself. He is at the mercy of fortune. Modern man's substitute for Fate is largely to be found in those dehumanized mass forces which sweep peoples into depressions, totalitarianism and war. The greatest threat to human existence is no longer nature; to an enormous extent science has made it possible to use nature for human ends. The greatest threat is man himself—his untamed irrational drives, his cruelty, his capacity for collective self-deception and mistrust.

Among the expedients available, aside from "education," there are only two which can *directly* transform man's internal character-structure; only two which can thus assist him to bring forth from within himself the resources for changing the patterns of contemporary civilization. Those two resources are psychotherapy and religion. Quite conceivably they may not succeed. Indeed, it is somewhat ironical that psychologists, anthropologists and sociologists are reaching conclusions about how to *design* a culture intelligently at the very moment when rapidly moving events may forever shut off the opportunity for putting their knowledge into practice.

Whether world civilization survives the present crisis or not, the stress upon the word "directly" in the above statement is necessary because under pressing circumstances men show an amazing capacity for unplanned, undirected adaptation. They can make adjustments to new and staggeringly different modes of life, which lead to profound changes in character and motivation, without deliberately attempting to alter themselves inwardly at all. Unless there were these hidden resources for meeting emergencies human life probably would have vanished from the planet long ago. But the tenacity and ingenuity with which human beings have managed to keep their history going should not lull us into an underestimation of present perils. For one thing, cultures do manage to wither up or to destroy themselves. And for another thing, the transition which men are called upon to make today is, so far as we can see, quite unprecedented. Evolution has produced a few crucial "leaps"; one where life emerged and gained a foothold; another where rational self-consciousness developed and managed to maintain itself. But never before have men had the power to destroy, not only their own civilization, but every prospect of a future re-establishment of the human enterprise. Therefore, no matter how great the positive contributions of science and religion have been in the past, they may not be able to provide us with answers adequate for the present. But it does not follow that we should leave matters to chance, in the blind faith that "evolution" or "man's fundamental will-to-live" or his intelligence or his goodness will enable us to rise to the emergency somehow.

Finally, wherever individuals can be helped to make a transition from misery to beatitude, then such help is worth-while in itself, whether civilization is headed for progress or catastrophe. The curing of psychological and spiritual ills makes a direct contribution to the building of a better world; but one does not have to believe that the advent of this better world is either possible or likely in order to justify such cures. Assume for the moment that civilization is doomed. It is still possible for individuals to move against this sickness; it is possible for them to achieve integrity and serenity (though not without tragedy) in their own lives; it is possible for them to continue spreading health as rapidly and widely as circumstances permit. No one can predict whether the influences that make for stability, co-operation and sanity *can* spread powerfully enough to hold in check and overcome the influences that are making for destruction. But no man can ask to foresee the ultimate outcome of his work, especially as it affects future generations; one can do no more than work for the betterment of human life here and now, without guarantees concerning the outcome.

CHAPTER II

The Need for Therapy

THERE ARE SO many books on mental illness, written for the layman, that any attempt here to give a detailed account of neurotic and psychotic disorders would be superfluous. It is necessary, however, to give a general sketch of the factors with which the psychotherapist has to deal in treating emotional conflicts. Otherwise it will be impossible to discuss how he goes about his task, what he is trying to accomplish, and why his methods are successful.

Recent studies have shown that a culture tends to develop basic patterns of child training, marriage customs, economic cooperation and competition, religious rites, etc., which fit together into a more or less consistent constellation. These patterns have a direct, momentous bearing upon individual character. In one instance they can insure that most members of a tribe, from generation to generation, will be self-reliant and emotionally secure; in another instance a very different set of cultural patterns will produce a high degree of anxiety and hostility. If these observations are right, they indicate that the mental health of the individual depends upon conditions that—in principle, at least —are alterable. Earlier psycho-analytic thought sounded a definitely fatalistic note insofar as it attributed to man an instinctual equipment which had to be combated by society and the individual's own conscience in order to maintain any kind of stable civilization. The difference between the older and the newer view can be expressed quite simply. In the one case civilized man is fated by his very nature to be torn inwardly by serious conflicts. In the other case such conflicts are related to modifiable circumstances; granted the establishment of favorable conditions, there is nothing in man himself which prevents him from reaching emotional stability and a satisfying use of his capacities.

To be sure, the newer view may not seem to offer much comfort. It says that if we can change contemporary society profoundly enough, we can reduce considerably the extent to which it drives people into anxiety, frustration, hopelessness and insanity. And the word "if" makes the whole statement discouraging. Nevertheless, this view makes a valuable contribution at two points even if one assumes pessimistically that it can do little to alter the present course of civilization.

In the first place it makes us aware of the fact that the health of the individual may involve resistance to surrounding cultural pressures at certain points, despite the fact that the latter are commonly regarded as due to "the way things have to be." In other words mental health cannot be defined *merely* in terms of adjustment, if adjustment means that the individual must indiscriminately fit into prevailing standards and assumptions. The success of a cure cannot be judged exclusively by whether he is enabled to function more comfortably within his social surroundings. There is a difference between the way in which a sick and a healthy person will rebel; but refusal to conform can be a sign of health. The events of the last few years have underscored the importance of these considerations. We need a view of human personality which would *not* define "mental health" within the Nazi state, for example, merely in terms of whatever enabled the individual to adjust to its principles with a minimum of internal tension and discomfort.

In the second place, the newer view prevents us from falling into illegitimate generalizations about human nature. By studying the causes of emotional disorder which have been prevalent in Western culture, we might be led to the mistaken conclusion that there is something in man as such which gives rise to these difficulties. Only a wider study, wherein we compare our own culture with others, can provide adequate grounds for discriminating between characteristics that are genuinely universal and those which reflect Western peculiarities. Unless we take this

point into account, our generalizations about man may be as
shaky as the generalizations about women which were reached
by a native in a tribe where most women had goiters; he assumed that susceptibility to having goiters and to having babies
were equally universal traits of femininity.

The most important discoveries of psycho-analysis have been
connected with the manner in which it has been able to gain
access to unconscious factors and to study their role in mental
conflict. Generally speaking, insofar as we are conscious of what
is involved in a conflict or tension, serious psychological harm
does not result. The situation may be painful, but it does not
tend to split us apart. For example, Mr. A has to choose between two positions, one of which offers a higher salary and the
other a more altruistic type of work. The considerations involved
are so delicately weighted that neither job is obviously and overwhelmingly more attractive. Mr. A goes through a considerable
amount of "mental torture" because of indecisiveness, inability
to foresee exactly how things will work out, and puzzlement as
to which advantage is more important. But because the "conflict" is due primarily to elements in the situation of which he
is aware, he resolves it in due course. He comes to terms with
the fact that he cannot have both jobs at once. He makes a
decision, and he feels that *he* has made it—that is, he accepts
responsibility for it.

But now let us put Mr. B—a "neurotic"—in the same situation. He will be unhappy no matter which decision he makes.
If he takes the more remunerative position he will feel guilty
for having been selfish; while if he takes the more altruistic position, he will feel discontented because of ambitions which are
left unsatisfied. He carries conflict within himself as a more or
less permanent condition, and it enters into every particular situation. To be sure, one position might aggravate his difficulties
more than another. But the basic fact is that he "doesn't really
know what he wants"—in work, or friendship, or marriage.

He *could* not be in this inwardly divided condition if he were

fully aware of the warring elements; but, in a sense, such awareness is the last thing he wants. In his attempt to find some sort
of harmony, Mr. B works out a rationalization whereby he takes
the position with the higher income while telling himself that he
is really choosing it from altruistic motives. He "protests" to
himself that what attracts him about the job is not so much the
salary as the opportunity for greater service through expanded
influence. No conscious hypocrisy is involved. As his acquaintances put it, "Mr. B is blind to his real motives." Yet his "selfish"
motives do not cease operating merely because he is unconscious
of them. Besides determining his choice of a job, they color all
of his human relationships and underlie everything he is striving for. Mr. B has the happy faculty of being oblivious to any
motives which do not fit into an exalted picture of himself; yet
this "happy faculty" is directly connected with his continuing
unhappiness.

In everyday experience we continually encounter people like
Mr. B. When they are driven into a corner and compelled to
recognize something about themselves which they regard as unworthy, the usual reaction is one of anger or stubborn denial.
Insofar as they are truly unconscious of these rejected forces
(that is, insofar as they have repressed them), they do not include them in a picture of their "real selves." Yet repression
means that these same forces continue to operate behind the
scenes instead of being brought into the open where they might
be dealt with more effectively. Ordinarily, however, it does not
help a neurotic person at all to tell him the plain truth about
the most discreditable parts of himself. His natural, and partly
justified, annoyance concentrates attention so exclusively upon
defending himself against criticism that he is in no condition to
ask himself calmly whether what the critic says is true. And, in
any case, a critic is the last person in the world to whom one
is willing to make a confession.

We have now seen in a preliminary way that there is an important difference between "conscious" conflicts, and those which
involve unconscious factors. When we are aware of putting aside

or restricting an impulse, that is called "suppression." We deliberately relinquish or limit a given desire for the sake of serving a purpose which we regard as worth the cost involved. By and large, suppression does not cause psychological harm. For the sake of aims which they whole-heartedly espouse, people can put up with a considerable amount of inhibition, inconvenience and sacrifice without falling into mental illness. Their lives may even be deeply tragic in many respects, but they are not "broken." However, when we reject an impulse in such a way that we are largely or wholly unconscious of it, that is called "repression," and, by and large, it is harmful. As we have seen, one does not necessarily stop wanting something "unworthy"—or "noble," for that matter—merely by becoming unconscious of the fact that he wants it. Yet so long as the impulse remains unconscious and unsatisfied, it can cut athwart the conscious aims of the individual and work against what he thinks he wants to become.

Another example will serve to bring out the difference between suppression and repression. Mr. X, a college student, is trying to write a term paper which is due on Monday. There is a house party scheduled for the week-end, and he wants very much to go to it, but he knows that he must choose between the paper and the party. Since he really "wants most" what can be gained by finishing the paper—completion of the course, leading to graduation, leading to professional training—he has to suppress his desire to go to the house party; this pains him deeply, but he can stand it. In fact, he even succeeds in finishing the paper by Monday morning.

Now contrast his situation with Mr. Y, who is conscious of nothing except a burning desire, not merely to finish his term paper on time, but to get as high a grade as possible. Because he is shooting for Phi Beta Kappa, Mr. Y has not even given the house party a second thought. His entire attention is centered on graduation, professional training and brilliant success in later life. So he sits down in front of the typewriter—and nothing comes. His mind is a blank. He tears up page after page and throws them into the waste-basket. He smokes too much.

He goes over to the window and stares out at the campus. Since Mr. Y is not aware of what is blocking him we shall have to go behind the scenes to find out. From earliest childhood he has discovered that by being bright he could obtain approval at home and recognition for achievement. Since he is not athletically inclined and not at ease socially, all of his energies have gone into the one way in which he can excel. His father is a doctor, and, ever since he can remember, it has been taken for granted that he would some day follow in his father's footsteps and take over the practice. Yet it is as though voices which he cannot hear speak inside him, saying: "If you don't make a high grade, you will be regarded as a failure at home, and you won't amount to anything on campus. So the term paper must be perfect. But you can't write a perfect paper. It's an impossible task. You'll slave away, missing all the fun of college life, and what will you have to show for it? You don't really want to be a doctor. You don't like chemistry and biology. You much prefer English literature and you'd like to be a writer, but your father says that nobody can make a living as a writer unless he's a genius or a Communist and you're neither. So you have to slave away, working for something you don't really want, driven by a fear of failure which keeps you constantly straining to reach an impossibly high standard." Mr. Y's mind goes blank because his heart isn't in the term paper, even though all his conscious intentions are. The task he has set for himself—namely, the achievement of perfection—is so impossible that he can't even get started. He is paralyzed by fear of not doing well enough, paralyzed so that he cannot use his knowledge of the subject even though it is superior to that of most of those in the class. He would like to have some of the fun that the house party symbolizes, even though he has not given it a second thought.

Notice that among the significant differences between the two men, Mr. X is not at all puzzled when he finds it hard to get the house party out of his mind so that he can concentrate, whereas Mr. Y "can't figure out" why his mind goes blank on him when he knows the subject adequately.

How does harmful (neurotic) conflict get started? In the family situation; but well-nigh everything, healthy as well as unhealthy, gets started in the family situation. Even though we must recognize fully the terrible emotional harm which parents may do their children, often through inadequacies in themselves which they cannot remedy merely by acquiring information or by making an effort, we must also remember that without support from adults the human child would be peculiarly helpless. He cannot start fending for himself at an early age, because he has so much to learn. Among the things he has to learn is some sort of orientation toward a heritage of language, scientific knowledge, and moral, æsthetic and religious traditions which must be transmitted through the development of persons. The human child enters the world with an equipment which develops slowly, so far as taking care of physical and biological needs is concerned, because he is so delicately and richly endowed for entering into a heritage that animals cannot possess. Therefore the long period of relative helplessness and slow growth, which opens the way to all the perils of being "injured" by the parents upon whom the child is dependent, goes hand in hand with the possibility of achieving full human status. We cannot have the high potentialities of human nature without the attendant risks. If the goods of a cultural heritage must be transmitted through the development of each new person, then evils—emotional disorders, prejudices, unjust social and economic patterns, deeply rooted national hatreds—can be transmitted and perpetuated in the same way.

Another risk arises from the fact that human beings are poor, as compared with animals, in instinctual equipment because intelligence is destined to play such a dominant role. What a human baby lacks in comparison with a homing-pigeon, an ant or a fox, he eventually makes up for a thousandfold. An instinct "works" for an animal only so long as the environmental conditions to which it is suited remain relatively stable; if things go wrong only a few of the higher animals can employ a measure of problem-solving in getting themselves out of the predicament.

But man is able to remember the past, anticipate the future, understand causal connections, employ universal notions, follow out logical implications, adapt himself to an infinite variety of changing circumstances, identify himself as a self-conscious person distinct from others, organize his communities by means of symbols and ideas, and enrich his life through creative imagination. One cannot have these potentialities without increasing the number of ways in which things can go awry. From the point of view of producing, maintaining and enjoying a cultural heritage, human consciousness is utterly indispensable. But from the point of view of fitting neatly into the endless round of nature's cycle—birth, struggle for survival, instinctual routine, maturation, reproduction, and death—human consciousness might almost be described as a nuisance. Indeed, the Spanish writer Unamuno has (fancifully) ascribed its origin to an ape with a peculiar cerebral disease. Yet it is this "disease" which makes man a center of good and evil. Nature can afford to be heedless of the individual; man injures his "human-ness" if he becomes thus heedless. Animals kill when they are hungry or threatened; but man can kill with calculated cruelty, and instead of killing physically he can violate the mind, the personality, of another. Whereas an animal can be only an animal, man, because he has the potentialities just described, can fall into physical and moral caricatures of his own nature; he can miss, in important respects, what it means to be human; he can become worse than an animal.

We must keep these special perils and special capacities in mind as we glance at the family situation. In our culture emotional conflict frequently arises where, because the child is born into a highly competitive society, the parents tend to value him not for what he is in himself but in terms of the prestige that the child can bring them by developing certain traits and skills. Moreover, the parents are inclined to judge the child by standards which they merely wish they fulfilled, or think they ought to fulfill, or imagine they fulfill. Hence as he grows up the child feels pressed not only to measure up to their attainments but to make up for their lacks. He must be a certain way—"or else." The "or else" carries with it an unspoken threat; he will be deprived of the affection and the sense of belonging which are quite indispensable to his own growth. It is almost impossible for a small child to hold out against such a threat.

Some may be inclined to deny the last statement. What about the child who is deliberately naughty? Is this not an instance of being able to risk the loss of affection? Yet the child's "naughtiness" is certainly not aimed at bringing about this loss. He may have natural curiosities which come into conflict with the convenience of adults, but these should not be labeled "naughty." From the mother's standpoint a curtain is something to hang neatly in the window; from the child's standpoint it is something nice to chew. From the father's standpoint, a book is something to be read and cherished; from the child's standpoint it is something nice to tear up. In such cases the child is not, in the first instance, "rebelling" against anything; he is simply following his own lines of force. When he endangers life, limb and (some forms of) property, he has to be stopped or distracted, and then rebellion may ensue; but if he is placed in circumstances where he can follow his own inclinations without running risks that cannot be permitted, there will be nothing to feed the rebelliousness. Even when such circumstances cannot be devised, the rebelliousness will not take hold as a more or less permanent disposition so long as the necessary restrictions are accompanied by adequate affection from the parents. Most "deliberate" naughtiness is not an attempt to alienate affection; it is a groping attempt to make up for the lack of it. Usually it is aimed at getting attention—which might be translated as obtaining the assurance that somebody cares. Yet after all these explanations have been accepted, there may seem to be a residual "orneriness" in some children which remains unaccounted for; the one thing we can be sure of is that insofar as this goes beyond a healthy will to live, which may have to take vigorous forms in some environments, it manifests a need to "get back" at parents or others. Instead of simply attributing orneriness to the child, we should ask what he needs to "get back" at.

A general establishment of stable limits within which behavior is channeled is just as essential to the child's sense of security as outlets for self-expression; but in order to be effective, these stable limits must reflect what is appropriate to the child's stage of development, instead of the fixed ideas (or the whims) of adults. Insofar as parental demands spring from an unconscious need to compensate for lacks in themselves by means of the child, there is no way of making sure that these demands are appropriate to his growing, and unique, individuality. They are like rigid moulds into which he is forced to fit. Of course the child is not aware of what is wrong, any more than the parents are. Only as he grows old enough to compare his lot with those of others can he begin to "get a bead" on what is satisfying or unsatisfying in his own family situation, and even then he may be so closely identified with it that it seems normal to him and any departures from it strange. Often it is only after one has become an adult, with considerable experience of diversified patterns of living, that one can look back upon his own parents and trace adequately within himself what they have "done to him;" and such a retracing of the past does not usually occur on a full scale outside psycho-analysis. As Jung has pointed out, some middle-aged men do not finally discover their own personalities until their fathers die; then a sudden spurt of maturing occurs, as though the man realized for the first time that he was really grown up and capable of making independent decisions instead of having to worry about what the "old man" would think of him.

In any case, a child can never grow easily into maturity and responsibility so long as standards are merely imposed upon him instead of being made authentically his own, and "authentically" involves having the support of his spontaneous motivation. Many homes make the pathway from infant dependence to full maturity anything but easy and gradual. Initially its standards are like the atmosphere the infant breathes. As he becomes aware of them he finds out what it means to be good and bad in the course of doing things that are praised and blamed. Eventually he begins to judge himself in terms that are thus intimately related to the idiosyncrasies of his parents. That is why it is so crucially important that the parents be capable of valuing the child for himself instead of as an extension of their own egos; and this capacity in them depends upon their total orientation to life; it depends especially on whether they are secure enough to operate in a "live and let live" fashion, or whether they are compelled by their own insecurities to follow a rule of "dominate or be dominated."

Probably "standard" is not a very good word for what is being described at this point. It connotes deliberate intention and reflection, whereas, as has just been indicated, strong emotional reactions and unconscious needs play an important part, along with consciously acknowledged norms and ideals. Needless to say, the child is affected much more by what the parents feel than by what they say. One can call a child "a nasty little brat," and if affection lies behind the words he will be aware of that —whether he understands the words or not. On the other hand, one can say: "Oh, darling, darling" to him in the sweetest tone imaginable—before company, for example; but if anger lies behind the words he'll feel *that*. If the parents have had a quarrel and are furious with each other, they may carry on a polite conversation at the dinner table; but what will "register" with the child, directly and painfully, will be the unspoken antagonism, the atmosphere of taut resentment. He will not be deceived by the polite words and tones.

The process whereby the parents' views and reactions become internalized in the child is a fateful one. He is in no position to accept or reject his own traits on an objective, discriminatory basis. In general he has to accept those things in himself which tend to evoke the responses he needs from the parents, and to reject those things in himself which evoke threatening or disturbing reactions from them. Where either parent, because of emotional blockages, is incapable of real affection, the child is in a difficult spot. He may resort to pathetic forms of ingenuity in seeking to obtain recognition, approval and warmth—all to no avail; and he may feel obscurely that the fault somehow lies with him instead of the parent. To make matters worse, the deficiency in real warmth is sometimes accompanied by an exaggerated display of affection, especially on the part of the mother. This is emotionally confusing to the child, and although of course he cannot describe his confusion verbally, it takes the form of being puzzled as to why so much "love" leaves him empty and unsatisfied.

One could illustrate indefinitely the variety of ways in which the definition of what it means to be a "good little child" or a "bad little child" becomes internalized in a manner which reflects the personalities of the parents. If the father is domineering, being "good" may be synonymous with "hopping" when he speaks. If the mother is excessively neat and orderly, then being "good" may be synonymous with playing quietly, keeping out of dirt, and not touching things on tables. These definitions get indelibly worked into the child's character long before he is in a position to discriminate between reasonable obedience and frightened submission, or reasonable orderliness and finicky neatness. That is one of the reasons, among several others, why late adolescence is frequently a period of maximum tension between parents and children. The latter are learning to "debunk" the home standards and are beginning to find some of their own. They are discovering that what seemed initially like inescapable and normal laws of behavior, established by infallible and omnipotent adults, may turn out to be quite arbitrary, alterable, and even silly.

A large proportion of the self-rejection which takes place in the growing child is centered around his biological equipment in general and his sexual equipment in particular. Stupid handling of toilet training and of sexual curiosity is disastrous because repudiation of the body injures one's capacity for deep feeling, for affection, and for a sense of organic relatedness with nature and with other human beings. An especially baffling problem is posed by the fact that even when parents are intelligent about such matters they cannot safeguard the child from adverse surrounding influences. However, if he has been allowed to take a healthy attitude toward his own body, it may "roll off his back" when an old maid of either sex calls him "dirty" for manifesting the curiosities that are normal in growing children. At least his chances are much better than those of a child who grows up in a family where silence, embarrassment or severity surround the subject.

Since child-training is so largely the responsibility of the mother, a further word needs to be said about the emotional situation of American women. All too frequently, in our society, processes which fit and which unfit a woman for motherhood go hand in hand. For example, an advanced education may breed discontent with housework, diaper washing and long hours of looking after children. The woman feels that she is going to seed intellectually —and that she has no chance to use her college degree! Furthermore, the higher her sense of responsibility toward monogamy, the more she may have been brought up to regard sexual relations as slightly (or dreadfully) discreditable, and her own sexual urges as incompatible with civilized femininity. Some readers may feel that such remarks are at least two generations out of date. Especially since the disrupting effects of the war, the main problem is not that there are too many "nice," inhibited girls. Quite the contrary. And so far as the educated woman is concerned, the desire to have a life of her own, in professional work or community activity, is a far greater threat to doing a decent job of child-training than any sort of prudishness. Nevertheless it is still true that the conflict between being intelligent-and-idealistic and being "warm" is a real one for many women, especially for those brought up by mothers who were refined, puritanical and frigid. Even though the girls may have rebeled against this training, notably during the period when they managed to get married, the effects of it are likely to reassert themselves as they in turn take on the responsibilities of motherhood. With the threats to monogamous stability which exist today, it is not surprising if well-intentioned young wives, because of a desire to protect their daughters from a "wild" period and from divorce, should revert in part to the strategies of the preceding generation.

Insofar as a woman, for whatever reason, has not found an adequate sexual relationship with her husband, her children are sure to suffer. For this relationship is the indispensable basis for a normal development of all the other patterns of family affection. There is a tremendous difference between love directed toward the child on the part of an emotionally fulfilled woman, and "love" which puts pressure upon the child to make up for a gnawing lack in her life. In the former case, moments of correctional discipline or weary annoyance will not destroy the feeling that there is a living, inexhaustible spring of affection within the mother that can be counted on. In the latter case, anything which interferes with feeding the mother's need will be accompanied by a sense of guilt on the child's part, and a terrible, dark feeling of being cut off and rejected.

Perhaps we have been putting the cart before the horse in discussing the mother's relationship to the child, since the quality of the marriage precedes and in large measure determines that relationship. We cannot go into "marriage problems" at this point further than to say that the causes of failure in marriage are identical with the causes of failure in human relationships generally. This seemingly trite statement is worth stressing because so many young people look forward to marriage as a means of solving all the problems that they have been unable to solve otherwise. Yet the ability to let a mate have his or her own personality is dependent upon a general ability to let others lead their own lives. If a person has not reached self-possession apart from marriage, he is not likely to reach it by means of marriage; on the contrary, he is likely to "read into" the mate's personality qualities which would fit his own neurotic needs, and if these qualities are not forthcoming an endless tussle begins. One seeks to make the other overly dependent, or, conversely, to make the other carry the whole load. If the mate cannot or will not take on the desired role, then one feels that marriage has cheated him. Instead of being a relationship in which two emotionally mature persons facilitate each other's development, the marriage becomes a rigid, frustrating deadlock.

We have been tracing some of the main causes that contribute to the development of neuroses, and we can now summarize our findings by taking a cross-section glance at the neurotic personality. In so doing, we should remember that what we are dealing with are not static qualities; they are dynamic human resources which will get misused and thwarted if they do not have an opportunity to develop harmoniously. We shall organize our cross-section in terms of three interrelated factors, as Freud did. He called them the "super-ego," the "id," and the "ego," but we shall not confine ourselves precisely to what these terms connoted for him.

First, the standards by means of which the individual judges himself have become internalized in such a manner that they function, in part, automatically and unconsciously. They have been imposed upon him in ways that reflect the needs of his parents, or the adults who bring him up, instead of being fashioned to guide his own developing individuality. Therefore his own picture of what constitutes being "good" or "amounting to something" may be seriously out of line with his needs as a unique individual, and even out of line with what is indispensable to the psychological health of *any* child.

Secondly, rejected impulses do not cease operation merely by being excluded from consciousness; but so long as the conscientious part of the self has the upper hand, these repressed impulses are compelled to engage in a sort of running warfare. They may manifest themselves in disguised forms which can be explained away, so that the real significance of the manifestation is missed. They may sabotage what the conscientious part of the self aims at—as in the case of Mr. Y. Or they may occasionally break through the strait jacket which has been holding them down —as involuntary outbursts of rage, lust, etc. Yet besides being the source of the most unacceptable forms of behavior, this second factor is at the same time an indispensable portion of the individual's equipment for meeting danger, for taking initiative, for having a sense of bodily well-being, and for the giving and receiving of affection. Serious estrangement between these two parts of the self means that the latter is shut off from rational guidance and control. A person who is "split" in this fashion is likely to feel helpless because he *is* helpless. He does not have "on tap," for unstrained, directed employment, the resources without which one cannot be fully alive. His anxiety may be "free floating"—i.e., it can attach itself to almost any object and can be vaguely present when there is nothing in the situation of the moment to account for it. Rejected impulses are striving to get out and the person is anxious about what would happen if they succeeded in breaking through. Often this anxiety is well-founded in the sense that, because they have been held down, they can express themselves only in rebellious and destructive forms; and their eruption would threaten the internal unity of the self and its relations with other people.

Thirdly, there is the *ego,* which coincides with the individual's conscious picture of his own personality. If his conscientious standards function, for the most part, automatically and his repressed impulses drive him unconsciously, what power is left to the poor *ego?* Since we are drawing a cross-section of a neurotic personality, it is not surprising that the *ego* is in fact harried and squeezed. Such a person may feel as though his existence were at the mercy of external circumstances and internal forces over which he has very little control. Even persons who think that they are running their own lives, however, may actually have little capacity for determining their own actions and reactions. Standards which seem to issue from responsible reflection and spontaneous preference may be compulsive, and under such circumstances the neurotic structure tends to perpetuate itself; the feelings and impulses that run counter to these standards are so shut off from consciousness that no amount of reflection and weighing of ethical arguments will make them accessible.

What then prevents such a person from making perceptive moral judgments is not an incapacity to think straight, but an incapacity to feel in such a way that he takes in adequately what is involved for himself and others. Even the clearest, most cogent ethical principle can be empty and tyrannical unless it is accompanied by whole-heartedness ("feeling for self") and sympathy ("feeling for others").

We can describe a neurotic person, therefore, as one who is not free to be himself—fully, naturally and simply. Awareness of this lack of freedom may vary from acute consciousness of conflict to virtually complete obliviousness of it. And the conflict itself may vary in seriousness from being "tied up in knots" or "coming apart at the seams" to prosaic, stolid, low-voltage unhappiness. When an individual is not aware of the seriousness of his conflicts this may be due to the fact that he has projected them onto people or circumstances outside himself. Then the trouble always lies, in his opinion, with the wife, the boss, the world-situation, the Jews, the Communists, etc., and if these external annoyances could be straightened out, he assumes, everything inside himself would form a serene harmony.

Of course no sane person is so completely split that these three factors are entirely shut off from each other. There is a measure of internal unity or the individual could not function at all. As Karen Horney has shown, many neurotic structures can be explained as desperate attempts to hold the self together against the threat of complete disintegration. They are found in gifted people whose gifts make it difficult for them to adjust to the prevailing patterns of the surrounding culture; or in extremely sensitive people who are more seriously disturbed by unfavorable circumstances in childhood and in later life than the average person. Therefore, even though the neurotic structure may carry with it an enormous amount of unhappiness, hopelessness, wasted energy, thwarted talent and unsatisfactory relations with others, it may at the same time represent the best working compromise achievable—in the absence of professional psychotherapeutic assistance. And in some especially serious cases the alternative to the equilibrium of neurotic compromise may be complete disruption.

The residual core of unity which remains despite conflict is a major asset when the neurotic person turns to a therapist for help. The path to a cure lies in the direction of breaking down the wall of partition between the first and the second "parts" of the self which have just been described. Here again, however, words can be misleading. The relationship between these parts may be more like the interlocking pieces of a puzzle than a partition. They may fit each other so neatly, so ingeniously, that each sustains and reinforces the other, making it almost impossible to take the puzzle apart one piece at a time. For example, it is misleading to classify people into two seperate groups: those with "superiority" complexes and those with "inferiority" complexes. If the individual's estimate of his own abilities and limitations is seriously distorted, what one usually finds is that he possesses exaggerated ideas about himself in both directions at once. Delusions of grandeur form an interlocking relationship with feelings of inadequacy or worthlessness. The grandiose vision may come out in fantasy, as in that popular movie, "The Secret Life of Walter Mitty"; or it may be associated with a vague, less technicolored conviction that some day he'll "get a break" or "show them." Distortions in self-evaluation may delay indefinitely coming to terms with one's actual position in life and obtaining the satisfactions which only then are available. On the other hand, they may be the sole means of keeping a man going, so that if his fantasies were dispelled (without at the same time enabling him to develop the latent resources which have been blocked by the neurosis) he would be left with an unalleviated feeling of worthlessness and hopelessness. In our own times we have seen what can happen when millions of "little men" in a frustrated and hopeless nation identify themselves with a symbolic "little man" (who also happened to be a malevolent genius). When actual circumstances are so confining and discouraging that the individual cannot find a meaningful life by means of his own strength, then one "way out" is to escape into collective fantasy. And by means of collective fantasy, as we all know, the Nazis released subrational potencies which came perilously near turning the dreams into fulfillment.

Another instance of the interlocking of seemingly contrary traits can be found in the person who is extremely polite, obliging and eager to be liked, but who underneath is intensely hostile toward those upon whom he makes himself dependent. He may be quite unaware of these hostilities because he could not afford to run the risks of retaliation which would ensue if the slightest hint of his underlying attitude appeared. The familiar experience of wondering why we are not grateful enough toward those who help us illustrates this ambiguity. The "unworthy" resentment may be due to the fact that we secretly regard receiving help of any kind as humiliating; it may be due to the fact that the helper is unconsciously trying to gain too much power over our lives. The relevant point is that an outer crust of gratitude may cover an inner core of resentment.

One other example. The person who is rigidly dogmatic in his opinions and always has to be in the right is not only bound to be insecure at some level, he is likely to be most uncertain (unconsciously) of his own opinions in precisely those areas where he is most dogmatic and easily aroused. The rigidity is a sign that the beliefs in question perform a function which is emotionally important to him; they are a means whereby he holds himself together *against* reality, or some aspects of reality. If his whole self, including his feelings, were based on something unshatterable, he would not have to argue himself and others into continually bowing before the rightness of his opinions. Instead of having to twist every available bit of evidence and every process of logic into the support of his views, he would welcome opportunities for co-operative testing and correction of them.

We need to remind ourselves that the examples just offered are meant to illustrate internal conflict. It goes without saying that there are people whose actual abilities and accomplishments support quite high views of their own status without giving rise to the suspicion that they are compensating for a sense of inferiority or helplessness. Winston Churchill is not indulging in a delusion of grandeur if he regards himself as an eloquent orator. Similarly there are people who are unambiguously kind, and whose friendliness springs from a genuine love of people instead of from a fear of being disliked or criticized. Finally, there are people who are steady and firm in their allegiance to convictions, not because they submerge doubts and ignore evidence to the contrary, but because their convictions are a straightforward expression of continually tested and confirmed experience, and it would be hypocritical on their part to pretend that they believed differently.

This chapter has stressed the fact that inward conflict is so directly related to estrangement from others that whatever intensifies one will intensify both. Because most of us do not have an adequate opportunity in family life, in school, in business and in community relationships to "be ourselves," we develop false fronts which conceal the truth concerning our own behavior and motives from ourselves as well as from others. For obvious reasons, the home is the natural starting-point for an inquiry into how character and emotional disorders develop, but we should remind ourselves that the home reflects the culture. In addition to the moral demands already described, the individual's sense of security and personal worth are also profoundly affected by how he fits into the economic and social patterns in terms of which success is judged. And, especially after adolescence, conflicts which arise in relationship to these latter demands can be so isolating and enslaving that they call for special comment. Many lives which seem to be quite well-adjusted to prevailing American patterns must nevertheless be regarded, from a psychotherapeutic standpoint, as impoverished and immature.

Consider, for example, a salesman who is so intent upon closing a deal successfully that he has no personality of his own. He smoothly toadies to the domineering customer, agrees with his prejudices, apes his moods. He plays the role so automatically that he has lost touch with his own reactions. Then when the

salesman gets home his unconscious resentment toward the customer and the demands of the job comes out in a flare-up of
temper at his wife and children. A trivial incident occurs to
which a mild objection would be appropriate, but instead of
making a protest geared to the incident, he shouts. His resentment has been displaced from the customer to his family. His
job dominates him so continually that he needs to dominate
somebody in turn. In the outside world he will get disliked or
slapped down if he asserts himself; but behind the closed doors
of his house he can let himself go, and he can "rule the roost"
because he brings home the pay checks.

This illustration serves to point up several questions which
have a bearing upon the difference between a healthy and a
neurotic orientation. Does the individual have a consistent personality of his own which he carries into all relationships, or is
he like a chameleon? Is he in touch with his own feelings and
reactions so that he can express them or withhold them as he
sees fit, or is his consciousness of them determined by whether
the circumstances make it safe to have them then? Are his responses, when he makes them, appropriate to what evokes them,
and directed toward what evokes them? Does he take responsibility for his own resentments, fatigue, compromises and failures, or does he try to shift the load onto others? Is he open in
his relations with fellow human beings, insofar as they are capable of responding perceptively to this openness, or does he involuntarily live behind a mask, see only the mask which others
wear, and thus fail to get through to them?

Any one who considers these questions carefully will realize
the extent to which our culture makes for "phony" relationships
—and for "phony" people as they grow up in these relationships. Unfortunately the conditions surrounding success tend to
intensify the problem. The "rules of the game" force us into
moulds and force us to deal with others in terms of impersonal
formulæ. Naturally competence in any profession requires that
the handling of secondary matters shall be routinized, in order
that a larger measure of energy and attention may be freed for

dealing intelligently and sensitively with primary considerations. But we prevailingly reverse the proper order. We routinize our own personalities and our dealings with others so as to make them serve the rules of efficiency, instead of routinizing our handling of externals so as to make them serve the ends of human freedom.

Under such circumstances, the building up of a false front is for many people an indispensable means of maintaining security. They receive acceptance, prestige and monetary rewards in return for being the kind of person who fits in with the dictates of a business concern, a social class, a community. Anything which does not coincide with this role is regarded by the individual himself as dangerous. He represses not only his "immoral" impulses, but those impulses which would interfere with his being a cog in a machine. If recalcitrant forces do manifest themselves, the primary inclination may be to get rid of them or bring them under control as quickly as possible. In any event, there seems to be no way of using them constructively; they are merely disturbing. The person who is set on getting rich has an odd, flashing moment of feeling that his aims are essentially empty and that he is missing what he really wants. The puritanical blue-stocking has an odd, flashing moment when he realizes that he is enjoying the profane novel or the naughty show he is engaged in censoring. The ruthless criminal who doesn't trust anybody, has no nerves and no sympathies, nevertheless has a sudden feeling of helplessness, terror or longing for decency. In all these instances the element which does not fit must be brushed aside for the sake of retaining the internal consistency which has enabled the individual to cope with the kind of life he has fallen into.

Another way of handling such internecine warfare is to compartmentalize the self. The growing child may discover that it is expedient to be one way at home and another way outside; with his parents he is docile, but with the gang he's a terror. By shifting gears he obtains approval in both quarters. At the adult level a familiar form of compartmentalization is found in the man who is tough in business but kind to his family. There are even people who regard it as an interesting "enrichment" of life to violate in some situations what they affirm in others—for example, to be scrupulously truthful in talking with men, but unbridled liars when trying to get the better of women. The discrepancies which attend a compartmentalized life would make the individual dizzy if he could take them in all at once. He would be confronted by the fact that what he has palmed off as an enrichment is really an impoverishment, a simple lack of integrity. Instead of saying, "I don't know what to make of myself" jestingly, he would have to recognize the grim implications of that statement.

As we shall see in the next chapter, psychotherapy must, in important respects, "swim against the cultural stream" in attempting to turn human resources away from the conflicts just described. Against the pressures which drive men in the direction of becoming automata, it aims at enabling them to accept or to resist these pressures responsibly. Against the artificialities and estrangements which isolate men from others (no matter how many good "contacts" they may have), it aims at enabling them to give precedence to warmth and genuineness in human relationships over the business advantages and social prestige they may bring. Against the pseudo-integration which achieves singleness of purpose by "holding down" parts of the self, it aims at unification of the whole self. Against the compromise of living in compartments, it aims at an over-all integrity.

Without entering into theological questions at the moment, it should be obvious from such a summary that these psychotherapeutic aims are compatible with the aims of sound religion. It is also well to note one of the reasons why neurotic disorders and interest in religion are sometimes found together. The person who can "adjust" comfortably to a thin, externalized existence will not feel the need for a deeper orientation, and he is not likely to get sick. Needless to say, a great many of these "adjusted" people are church members, and their participation in religion, like their participation in everything else, reflects the thinness and externalization of their lives. Psychotherapists have long recognized that a neurosis can be a blessing in disguise; for it can prevent a person from settling back into a narrow, obtuse, humdrum organization of his life, and compel him, in the course of seeking to get rid of his unhappiness, to "break open" into a more complete employment of his own vitality and insight. Often people for whom religion has been a matter of intense, shattering personal experience, instead of a matter of conventional observance, have been "neurotic" in the sense that they have been driven to seek deeper orientations than those provided by the "closed" society in which they lived. This does not mean that all the religious solutions they have reached have been equally valid. When religious fantasies are used to consolidate a neurosis they can produce "remedies" worse than the disease they are supposed to cure. Nevertheless, it is also true that fruitful struggle to cope with and to overcome inner conflict may drive a man into the deepest levels of religious awareness and understanding.

CHAPTER III

How Therapy Works, and Why

WHY DOES PSYCHOTHERAPY work? The simplest answer is that it provides a situation in which a person can be completely honest with himself and with a fellow human being. Conversely, it provides a situation in which he can discover how much he has deceived himself hitherto; the manner in which his ideal picture of himself, his unrecognized needs, and his special way of trying to make the universe conform to his private demands, have caused him to distort reality. "Reality" is, of course, a contentious word for philosophers. Here it is intentionally used in a quite unsophisticated way. We distort reality, for example, when our own suspiciousness prompts us to attribute unfriendly attitudes to friendly people; or when we equate timid submission and flattery with "love"; or when we avoid recognizing our own inadequacies by claiming that others have stacked the cards against us.

Usually it is futile to try to estimate how much such distortion is deliberate and how much it is involuntary. Think of some one deeply entrenched in racial prejudice. Is his bias due to the fact that he *will* not see through it or *can* not see through it? In any case, self-deception can be removed only by becoming able to detect it as distorting; and this in turn involves acquiring some understanding of the needs which prompted one to fall into it in the first place.

This preliminary statement may look like a counsel of perfection. Who can ever become completely honest in the sense just described? Who can judge how far he has fallen short? The individual himself cannot, since he can never be sure that he has ferreted out all the unconscious sources of self-deception. A second person, seemingly, cannot; for he cannot have direct access to the inner life of the one he is trying to judge. And how can this second person be sure that his own judgments are not distorted?

These obstacles, which theoretically are insuperable, do indeed make the psychotherapeutic task difficult, but they do not make it impossible. They may serve to remind us that the goal is a flying one. Probably no one reaches perfect integration, if that means harmonious awareness of all the forces that are at work in the self, and capacity to deal responsibly with them. And even if one did reach it for a moment, the next moment would contain the possibility of lapsing away from it. As long as life lasts, each person is continually confronting new problems, new possibilities of failure; some powers are coming to fruition while others are diminishing or falling into discard. Therefore mental health depends upon adequacy to cope with ongoing processes and situations; it depends especially upon openness to fresh experience whereby the individual may continue to move forward in self-understanding and in understanding of others. It is not a finished, fixed state.

In the literature concerning mental illness, the materials which furnish an account of neurotic and psychotic disorders are much more clear-cut and definite than those which deal with the techniques of healing. (This statement applies, of course, only to psychotherapy, not to techniques such as electro-shock or insulin.) The reason for this seeming discrepancy is simple. A general account of "our inner conflicts" covers tendencies and traits which, in various ways, are operative in everyone. But the healing process, if it is to be effective, must be "tailor-made" to fit each individual. Certain basic principles can be laid down; but everything depends upon the way in which the patient and the therapist incorporate these principles in the particular relationship which they establish with each other. Even after reading a complete transcription of the conversations that went on in the course of a psycho-analysis, one may feel that something essential has eluded the printed page. The feeling is right. Nothing less than the full impact of one whole self in relation to another whole self can provide an adequate "sense" for what goes on; and, of course, in order to reach such a "sense" one has to participate in the relationship.

Granting adequate psychiatric training and experience, here are some of the skills which vary with the personality of the therapist: ability to form an accurate over-all impression of the individual he is working with; ability to move from a general knowledge of the dynamics of normal and abnormal psychology to an illuminating application in the particular case; ability to penetrate behind the appearances, the tone of voice, the incidental gesture, the seemingly trivial details, to what is going on in the other person; ability to grasp intuitively (though on the basis of hard-won, text-book knowledge) how apparently unrelated items fall together into a pattern; ability to interpret dreams; ability to anticipate crises and turning points. Most of all, the therapist's effectiveness depends upon his ability to detect his own limitations—lack of sympathetic insight, inability to be sufficiently objective, involuntary ways of "using" the patient to fulfill his own needs.

We must acknowledge, therefore, that our general description in this chapter of how and why therapy works, will inevitably abstract from the most essential feature—namely, a person-to-person relationship in its full concreteness. Obviously such a relationship cannot be described "generally." It is lived through uniquely by each individual who experiences it.

The conditions described in Chapter II, which make psychotherapy necessary or desirable for so many human beings in this "age of anxiety," are also, of course, the conditions which make the task difficult. In a sense, the therapist has to reverse the processes which have caused the harm. Praise and blame are put aside in order that *any* thought or feeling may be examined fully and freely. Whereas in most of his human relationships the patient is necessarily concerned about considerations of superiority and inferiority, here such considerations are eclipsed by the fact that both he and the therapist contribute what they can to a mutual enterprise; each plays an indispensable role, and competitiveness is pointless. The patient gradually learns that the aim of therapy, which is enhancement of his ability to understand himself and direct his own life, cannot be fostered by the methods he ordinarily employs. Aggressiveness is useless, since attempts to dominate the therapist will not succeed; he cannot be argued out of "seeing" whatever he does discern, though he is willing to enter into a mutual examination and testing of his insights. Compliance is useless, since one does not have to agree continually with the therapist in order to gain his approval; and attempts to get him to carry one about picky-back are gradually parried because they are incompatible with the aim of enhancing self-reliance. Aloofness is also useless, though it can be one of the most difficult obstacles of all to be surmounted; it may manifest itself as an inability to enter into deep emotions of any kind; it may take the even more subtle form of having and admitting many emotional reactions, but always as though from a distance. In any case, the therapy cannot really "get going" until the patient has been lured or blasted out of the citadel of detachment, so that he can identify himself fully with his own behavior and feelings and enter directly ("with his guard dropped") into the human relationship which the therapist offers. In ordinary life an individual not only has to be on the alert to defend himself or to "make a good showing" in social situations, he has to organize his thoughts as coherently and as acceptably as possible. This involves filtering out material which is irrational, childish, offensive, or banal. In the therapeutic situation, the patient is invited to express his thoughts as they come. In ordinary life, the person who faces serious emotional problems is usually isolated, no matter how many relatives and acquaintances he has, in the sense that he knows no one to whom he would dare communicate the nature of those problems. Therapy not only puts an end to such isolation; it offers the kind of reassurance which enables a person to move forward into painful and frightening forms of self-understanding he would not otherwise have the strength to face.

In a word, therapy offers a human relationship in which the

false-front is no longer necessary. Therefore it makes it possible to become aware of how false the front is and of what it is concealing. Though it is too early to make final judgments concerning the success of experiments in "self-analysis," we can see from the foregoing why it is usually impossible for a person to reverse the harmful processes all by himself. Psychological conflicts arise in connection with dynamic, emotional relationships with other persons. Therefore the most direct way of removing them involves replacing condemnatory, confining and artificial relationships with a form of human fellowship which embodies the opposite characteristics.

Often patients are very slow to believe that they have entered into a situation where they are not compelled to *be* a certain way in order to protect themselves or to gain approval. As the truth dawns on them, some have a wonderful feeling of release from life-long pressures; only then can they begin to see the difference between what they have been trying to make themselves be like and what they really want to be like. Others, temporarily, have a dreadful feeling of floundering; they have so long taken their cue from what was expected of them that when the cue is not forthcoming they do not know what to do with themselves; they feel rudderless, or as though they were falling through space. Some may feel that the therapist's attitude is immoral, and they may take it as sanctioning immorality on their part or they may feel that their own ethical standards are threatened by him. Others may feel that no human being can really be as permissive as the therapist seems, and they will continually attempt to read into his attitudes toward them the reactions they would have toward others under similar circumstances.

In any case, a human relationship in which one can be oneself, without fear of rejection or exploitation, is like an oasis in a desert for countless people. That fact must stand as a commentary upon our prevailing patterns of family life, friendship, economic success and church membership.

Since acceptance of the patient is the foundation of therapy, the misunderstandings which have arisen concerning it must be discussed. "Acceptance" does not mean that one fools himself into thinking that the patient is more lovable, harmless or noble than he is. It does not mean that value-judgments concerning the constructive or destructive consequences of a given action or character-structure must be suspended. It does not mean that the therapist must eradicate his own likes and dislikes. It does mean, however, that a noncondemnatory attitude is genuinely adopted, not merely "put on," because it facilitates the task. As we have seen, the task involves helping the patient to get his conflicts out into the open, to become aware of things which hitherto were unconscious, to understand the past and present functioning of anxieties and compulsions which have blocked him and made him feel guilty. If he were afraid to admit some things or to follow out the implications of what he was able to acknowledge, the widening of self-acquaintance could not occur. As a matter of fact, virtually all patients are surprised to discover how much they have automatically covered up because the inhibitions and restrictions of their social environment have become "a part of themselves."

Freud embodied the principle we have just described when he encouraged his patients to tell him everything that came into their heads, excluding nothing. The method of free-association, where one lets the mind run without reins, is a useful technique in this connection. (The popular caricature of psycho-analysis represents it as using what amounts to the *opposite* of free-association. The patient reports a carefully selected, "significant" happening or dream. Then the doctor, after consulting the textbooks on his shelf and much owlish pondering, proffers a highly complicated theory to explain the item in question.) When there is a hiatus—when, for example, one feels on the verge of saying something terribly important and his mind goes blank—that is a good indication that one has come upon buried material. Another major method for gaining access to such material is, of course, the interpretation of dreams. Discussion of this topic lies beyond the scope of a brief sketch. We cannot here attempt to adjudicate the dispute between Freud and Jung. The former developed an elaborate and ingenious theory to show that dreams speak a highly condensed, emotional language, but that even in sleep the "censor" which guards consciousness operates in such a way that the dream material has to disguise its full import. Jung assumes that dreams can mean exactly what they say, when they are properly understood. Despite these theoretical differences, many patients discover for themselves that a widening of what they are able to "take in" when they are fully awake goes hand in hand with an increasing ability to grasp what their dreams are saying. Sometimes, in the process of comprehending what the dream says they feel, they actually "feel that way," consciously, for the first time. Usually it is fruitless to attempt the interpretation of an isolated dream, offered by a person who is not engaged in analysis. But a cumulative sequence of dreams, when related to a process of widening self-understanding which can be checked by other means, can furnish valuable evidence concerning what is going on behind the scenes.

Therapists continue to use both free-association and the interpretation of dreams, but some of them have advanced beyond Freud at one important point. He was by no means free from authoritarianism in his approach to his patients. This was partly due to the fact that he was a pioneer who had to make his way against hostility and unfair criticism. Yet instead of simply leaving his patients free gradually to "catch on" to the techniques involved in analysis, he assumed that he had to break through resistance on their part. Undoubtedly some resistance is encountered in any analysis; but the time involved in treatment can frequently be shortened if the tussle is minimized instead of aggravated. After all, it is contradictory to try to *impose* a permissive situation upon a patient more rapidly than he wants it to develop. Unless he is allowed to follow his own pace in bringing out painful or humiliating material, he may go a few steps toward looking into the abyss of the unconscious, become panicky at what he dimly discerns, and then run away to hide behind an even higher wall of defensiveness.

The permissiveness of the therapist dispenses with praise and blame for the sake of getting at the full truth; but it is *not* an immoral attitude. Most psycho-analysts claim that it is an amoral attitude, essentially scientific in mood and outlook; but even that seems to me to be a half-truth. Karen Horney and Erich Fromm are right in contending that psycho-analysis deals with moral problems and seeks to serve moral purposes—provided that the word "moral" be properly understood. Every neurosis is a moral problem in the sense that it impairs the individual's happiness and robs society of the benefits which would flow from a creative use of his resources. Therapy has a moral purpose because it rests on the assumption that internal harmony and a capacity for personal growth and responsibility are better than emotional conflict, anxiety and self-enslavement. In serving this purpose it is fostering a humanitarian end which is analogous to religious salvation. Condemnatory attitudes are abandoned because clinical experience has demonstrated that they interfere with working intelligently and effectively toward the fulfillment of this purpose. In other words, the seemingly immoral or ethically neutral attitude has become central in the task of mental healing, not because the therapist does not care about how people live, but precisely because he is seriously concerned with enhancing personal integrity and emotional maturity.

There is no incompatibility between espousing aims which involve moral concern in this sense, and retaining a thoroughly scientific attitude, so long as the latter implies using all the available, tested knowledge of psychology or any other science in a manner which does not allow one's own desires to blind him to relevant facts or trick him into fallacious thinking. Only when the "scientific attitude" is equated with the dogma that all value-judgments and moral purposes are illusory or superfluous does a conflict arise. Much modern psychology, especially experimental psychology, has adopted this dogma in an effort to be as "scientific" as possible. Although psychotherapists can use the data furnished in studies by such psychologists, most of them find it impossible, in practice, to accept the views of human personality which follow from the dogma. The therapist is intimately acquainted with the manner in which biological, unconscious and conscious factors are woven together to form an internal character-structure. He must deal with the whole man as a psychosomatic unity. Therefore, although of course he realizes that the physical and biological laws which prevail throughout nature are operative in man, he does not (at least, he should not) make the mistake of assuming that human nature is merely the automatic resultant of the play of environmental forces. In interplay with his environment man strives for balance and wholeness, he responds and takes initiative, in ways which are not reducible to sub-personal phenomena.

The question of "free-will" is not being raised at this point; for the principles governing the operation of human character may involve thoroughgoing determinism, even though they cannot be formulated merely by generalization on the basis of the stimulus-response arc. Nor is the foregoing meant to suggest that man possesses a soul which is separate or separable from his body; indeed, traditional soul-body dualism is incompatible with the psycho-somatic approach just mentioned. The only point which is being urged at the moment is that therapy can combine a dispassionate scientific attitude with value-judgments and the service of moral ends. No one claims that such a combination is easy; but the actual practice and accomplishments of therapists prove that it is possible.

One further word of explanation is called for concerning the permissive attitude. Restrictions do have to be imposed whenever the possibility of carrying forward the therapeutic task would otherwise be imperiled. For example, although the patient may be allowed to say virtually anything under most circumstances, he cannot be allowed to continue indefinitely in wanton abusiveness toward the doctor. Even here, however, there is a difference between therapy and what usually happens in ordinary life. For abusiveness is dealt with, not by countering hostility with hostility, but by an appeal to the facts. The patient is offered an opportunity for entering into an adult relationship of mutual respect; if he wants to move forward into such a relationship, he must fulfill certain minimal conditions—not because the therapist arbitrarily demands this but because "the facts of life" demand it. Often, however, the problems connected with *overt* expression of hostility do not loom very large. The patient wants to be co-operative, and because he looks upon the doctor as his last hope he is exaggeratedly anxious not to antagonize him. Initially any resentment he may feel toward the man "who sits there in his well-integrated serenity and analyses my misery" is so well repressed that it does not come out violently except in dreams. The hostility involved is mixed with fear; the patient feels naked, or as though some one were taking pot-shots at him, or as though a surgeon were probing his wounds. (These examples are taken from actual dream material in which the figure of the therapist is identifiable.) In a good counseling relationship, by the time the patient can feel and express his antagonism freely, a mutual trust has grown up which ordinarily enables both participants to recognize its irrationality and inevitability.

Finally, the steady attempt to cut through rationalizations, evasions, projections and fantasies acts as a restricting influence in itself. Here again, however, the restrictions result not from arbitrary dictates on the part of the therapist but from the patient's own apprehension of reality as it collides with his desire to escape reality. Yet the doctor may have to exercise discretion. If the patient is living in a fool's paradise, thinking that he is successfully "getting away" with a line of conduct which is actually imperiling his existence, the therapist may have to "throw a scare" into him in connection with that specific matter —not by censure, but by an open-eyed appeal to the facts. There are no general rules as to when such fright will act as a beneficial stimulus and when it will lead to paralysis or headlong panic. Only long clinical experience, plus thorough knowledge of the individual case, plus, perhaps, an intuitive flair on the therapist's part, can give adequate guidance. Even then, the maxim "nothing ventured, nothing gained" still applies.

The combination of detached objectivity and participative

empathy which is called for on the part of the doctor is not easy to achieve. Indeed, successful completion and consolidation of his own psycho-analysis are indispensable prerequisites. But with practice, especially as he observes the actual consequences of success and failure in connection with such a combination, this "role" becomes natural and genuine. Some patients want too much warmth and construe any sign of detachment as hard-hearted. Others are excessively afraid of intimacy and regard any indication of human fellow-feeling as degrading or maudlin. Thus the therapist must possess a considerable degree of inner flexibility so as to adapt himself to the needs of the individual situation wisely. When good *rapport* cannot be established, he must be able to look for the explanation in his own limitations as well as in the illness of the patient. A combination of neutrality and receptiveness remains the best safeguard against being pulled about willy-nilly by the latter's neurotic needs. If, despite reassurance to the contrary, the patient persists in being afraid of getting the therapist "down" on him, the best device is to get that fear itself out into the open and to examine the reasons for its presence.

As we have seen, the therapist has standards of value by means of which he differentiates between illness and health, conflict and integration, creativity and sterility, growth and rigidity. They may not be formulated with conceptual finality; but they enter into his entire procedure, as flexible rules-of-thumb. However, it is an essential part of his view of human nature to recognize that the best results can be promoted only by helping the patient to develop his own standards of value, instead of imposing those of any one else upon him. Although this point can be stated with tolerable clarity, it is extremely difficult to fulfill in practice. There are powerful forces at work which impel the patient to cast the therapist into a normative role. Calmness, courage and honesty in the one may of course awaken and nourish the same resources in the other; but an illusory facsimile of these qualities can also be produced when the patient seeks to reach them by unconscious mimicry. Only unhurried analysis and complete candor can disclose the difference between development of genuine independence and parasitic imitation of the therapist's integration.

Because so much can be conveyed by a single tone, or a single silence, it is unwise to discount how much the individuality of *this particular therapist* in dynamic interrelationship with *this particular patient* may have a bearing upon the outcome. Even telepathy may be involved. Some observers have claimed that patients of Freudians tend to have Freudian dreams while patients of Jungians tend to have Jungian dreams. In any case, a person who has received some help from one doctor undoubtedly might have obtained more help from another. The same is true in medical practice generally, except that in psychiatry the personal equation plays a more decisive role. That is not to say that it does not play an important role in ordinary medical practice. The physician's personality *may* make little difference in the healing of a broken bone (though under some circumstances even this would not be true); it can make a great deal of difference to the ease of delivery in child-birth. Because the personal equation is so inescapable in psychiatry, many consultants gradually come to recognize the kind of patients with whom they can get maximum results and the kind for whom they are less suited. Sometimes a balky analysis can be expedited by referral to another doctor.

Nevertheless, any competent therapist can make such progress against the "garden variety" neuroses that he can usually get the patient into a position where he can navigate on his own. The latter then spends the rest of his life "completing the cure," after the consultations have finished. That is to say, he uses his released resources in a process of widening self-understanding and continual maturation which can go forward indefinitely. Sometimes the most gratifying results of an analysis do not appear until several years after its termination. When neurosis is the only obstacle, its resolution means that the person can continue to grow in wisdom, strength, joy and kindness to the day of his death.

Because there are so few competent therapists, in relation to the magnitude of the need, every labor-saving device is worth exploring. A few large institutes now steer the patient, on the basis of preliminary diagnosis, to the staff member best qualified to handle his particular case. The course of treatment is planned to fit the individual; the length and frequency of interviews, and the employment or avoidance of "transference," are matters to be considered flexibly. Various other innovations in group therapy, nondirective counseling (which largely excludes use of dream material), hypno-analysis and narco-synthesis have been tried, especially during and since the war. We shall not attempt to evaluate these experiments. Suffice it to say that psychiatry itself has introduced departures from the traditional "one hour a day, five times a week, for three years, at ten dollars a throw," which had put its services beyond the reach of all but the wealthy and the subsidized, and had severely limited the number of people whom one doctor could cure in the brief span of life allotted to him after completion of his lengthy training.

Yet if the preceding description of minimal requisites is sound, there is one circumstance which sets limits to any attempt to adopt mass-production methods. In the end integration, insofar as it is reached, must be "produced" by the patient himself. It consists in alterations of those modes of feeling, thinking and reacting which most intimately affect his attitude toward himself and others. Therefore, although the therapist knows general principles of mental health in advance, he does not know in advance what will constitute the maximum feasible achievement of mental health for any particular patient. Instead of trying to jockey the latter into fitting preconceived formulæ, the doctor must attempt to acquaint himself with the full concreteness and uniqueness of each personality he deals with. He cannot afford to forget that this living, striving human being is richer, more complex and more mysterious than any general concepts (no matter how sound). His procedure, therefore, is inductive and empirical; starting with immediate data, he moves forward to guiding concepts and general theories only as they serve the practical aim

of facilitating desirable changes. The criteria by which one esti-
mates the progress of the therapy must be tested and revised
continually, in the light of a constant return to the immediate
data. They must be tested not merely by whether they increase
the therapist's rational understanding of motives, but also by
whether they make possible an effective alteration of motivation
within the patient.

To ask which comes first, the immediate data or the evaluation, is a hen-and-egg question. The two go together. As acquaintance with the inner life of a particular patient widens, the
therapist's guiding criteria are confirmed, modified, or relin-
quished as inapplicable. Unless he had some idea of where he
was trying to go, he could not begin the task; but in order to
have at the outset a finished, fixed conception of maximum
achievable mental health for this patient, he would have to
possess magical foresight of all the responses, attitudes and actions which the latter will produce in the course of reaching this
desired goal. Therefore, he literally does not "have all the answers" concerning what constitutes the patient's beatitude; and
no one can have such answers for another person, for they are
empty (no matter how pretty or cogent they may be) until the
patient is enabled to fill them with the content of his own life.

We have already examined some of the cultural conditions
which explain why so many of us fail to discover that each
person must play a decisive part in achieving (or missing) beatitude by what he *is*. We seek answers to the meaning of life by
means of acquiring wealth, power, pleasure, popularity and any
number of other things. All of these things, so long as they are
external, leave us at the mercy of circumstances and in the
power of others. If the basis for the worth of a man's existence
does not lie within him, then the significance of his life can be
destroyed by forces beyond his control. The net result is deep-
seated anxiety. Such anxiety may cause endless attempts to
tighten one's grip upon property and power; but these expedients
can do no more than evade the problem; they cannot eradicate
it. Usually, the more desperately one places one's eggs in such

baskets, the more vulnerable he is. Feverish effort may drive a sense of emptiness and lostness out of consciousness; but the emptiness is therefore all the more acute at the core. The disruption is sure to be serious once strategies for keeping the emptiness out of sight have broken down. This sense of emptiness, lostness and isolation, which is so prevalent in contemporary life, is symptomatic of the fact that human resources for self-possession are not being adequately employed. Far too often we strive to meet the problem by *having* something significant instead of by *becoming or being* something significant.

It is quite amazing, once we have a chance to check on the matter, to discover how much of our time and energy goes into working for some one else, or for ends that we cannot wholeheartedly espouse. Exploration of the unconscious shows that, for many of us, what we regarded as our own choices in connection with selecting a job, or a mate, or a style of life, were actually dictated, in large measure, by forces of which we were not aware, and which we therefore could not direct or resist. The effort to "amount to something" in the eyes of parents or society—and, conversely, the effort to defy them—may go on operating behind the scenes in adult life long after the grown person has come to regard himself as completely independent. It may so color everything he admires and fears that his own spontaneous reactions are completely subordinated to automatic compliance and defiance.

In ordinary life we commonly seek to make people recognize things they do not want to see by forcing them to admit the truth. We tell them what they ought to know. We marshal irrefutable arguments. We give them "a good piece of our minds." But such methods do not give the "blind" individual an opportunity to be helped by an acknowledgment of the truth. In order for a man to become aware, with fully alert feelings, of things which were previously held out of consciousness because of their painfulness or their anxiety-laden qualities, his guard must indeed be broken through. But a head-on attempt to break through it results in a stiffening of his defenses, or a hasty retreat, or a humiliating capitulation. Confusion is caused by the fact that when some one else is trying to *force* him to see the truth, a struggle of wills ensues. Legitimate resistance against being dominated or humiliated is then used as a plausible excuse for resisting recognition of the truth.

Ideally, therapy avoids these mistakes. It breaks through a person's guard, not by an attack but by the opposite—by making it safe for him to drop his guard. The therapist recognizes that no matter how "right" he may be about things which the patient cannot or will not recognize, insistence upon this "rightness" leads to a Pyrrhic victory. The healing value of an insight is directly proportional to the degree in which the patient has made it his own instead of taking it over from another person.

The fact that most people with emotional problems deeply need a confidant, and find it an enormous relief to get things off their chests, facilitates the therapist's task. To be sure, some are initially so aloof, timid, suspicious or depressed that skillful preliminary work is called for before they can open up. But as good *rapport* is established, conflicts which have been bottled up for years come pouring out in early sessions.

We have already stressed the specialized training and the personal skillfulness which are requisite. Parenthetically we need to acknowledge again the harm that can result from the bungling of amateurs. For example, the silent patient may, so to speak, sit back and defy the consultant to "do something," or tacitly demand that he "do something." This situation does not ordinarily baffle the expert; he knows that the patient would not be there at all unless he had something he needed to talk about. But the amateur is likely to take the initiative prematurely. Even if he knows enough to refrain from trotting out advice, exhortation, and encapsulated "rules for living," he is apt to do far too much of the talking. He is likely to suggest "solutions" before he and the patient have carried through the painstaking spadework involved in getting the underlying problems out into the open. He is likely to keep the discussions too much at the theoretical level of *pondering,* and fail to establish an atmosphere where feelings can flow freely.

The implications of these parenthetical remarks would have to be followed out in considerable detail if our primary purpose were to discuss how pastors can increase their effectiveness in counseling. Suffice it to say at this point that the pressure of preaching and administrative duties, the expectation on the part of members of his congregation that he should be able to furnish ready-made answers, and the minister's own conception of his role in relation to religious truth, may easily lead to a style of "pastoral work" which seldom reaches to the roots of human problems. Similar considerations must be taken into account in appraising the value of radio programs and other popular devices for solving personal dilemmas. Who could be expected to carry through a quiet, unhurried, candid examination of his hidden motives and conflicts by means of ten minutes before a microphone on a nation-wide hook-up? Not all methods which use public confession or isolated, brief sessions with a psychological or pastoral "expert" are disreputable; but all of them need to be tested by the difference between (a) merely making people "feel good" or merely removing superficial symptoms, and (b) bringing about a permanent reorientation of character.

Now that some of the basic attitudes and approaches adopted in therapy have been described, a further examination of the course of the process itself should serve to make clear why shortcuts are likely to be dangerous or futile. The first reaction to "purgation" in an analysis is one of relief, as though a wound had been drained. Although we sometimes feel better after confessing to a friend, we can seldom be sure that he will keep our confidence, or that he will not use it against us, or that he will not think less of us because of what we have told him. A strict code of professional ethics surrounds the confidential character of psychotherapy; the troubled person can talk with freedom because he is not imposing on the time of the confidant (on the contrary, he is probably paying a stiff fee) ; and he either knows in advance, or quickly discovers, that, so far from being humiliated for telling his secrets, the utmost candor is an essential part of the procedure.

Frequently after the patient has begun to open up he has a delayed reaction. He finds that a much fuller revelation of his own ambiguities and weaknesses has come out than he had intended. If he has habitually maintained his poise by covering up feelings of shyness or worthlessness, and now these feelings have been exposed, he can no longer regain his poise by slipping it on like a garment. The therapist sees through him. The patient now has an opportunity for beginning to form a human relationship on a new and unfamiliar basis; but the desire to run for cover or to revert to the old strategies may be extremely intense. When a man's reputation and his good opinion of himself rest upon pretenses, he is loathe to relinquish the pretenses. Moreover, there may be plausible reasons for feeling at this point that the consultations have made him worse instead of better. His old self-assurance is gone. He began expecting that his problems would be solved by having various things changed in the external situation, and instead the process is moving in the direction of indicating that he needs to change himself. He sees no possibility of the latter change taking place, and he may even regard it as unnecessary and unjust. If the doctor would only give him specific rules to follow and actions to carry out, he would gladly do his bidding. But the way things are going, the patient is merely becoming conscious of the fact that his problems are more serious than he had thought at first; and *different* from what he had thought. They are not merely rooted in fate, or in the faults of others; they are rooted in himself. What he is staring at now is more insoluble than the dilemmas he came in with; and he has less drive, less confidence, to muster in meeting the emergency than ever before in his life.

This coming in sight of the underlying aspects of a problem can be so frightening or enraging to a person that he breaks off the analysis. He may not break it off in a forthright manner; he may not even recognize what he is doing. Instead, he may begin to come late to appointments, or forget them entirely; he may wake up with a cold on some of the days when he is scheduled for an interview; he may begin spending so much money on other things that he cannot afford the fees. There are numerous people walking the streets today who say that they tried psycho-analysis and it did not help them. Some gave it a full chance, and because of the incompetence of the therapist, or the seriousness of their own illness, or an inability of this particular patient to work effectively with this particular doctor, the result was a real failure. But many "bolted" at an early stage when they discovered that the analysis would involve hard, partly distasteful, work on their part instead of being a magical way of getting "fixed up." A high percentage of those who begin an analysis can be described as sincerely wanting to have all the inconveniences of their neuroses removed without relinquishing the neuroses themselves (Horney).

Fortunately, instead of running away entirely, many patients simply pass through one or more periods when they are unconsciously trying to sabotage the process of gaining further insight. These plateaus, when not much seems to be going on, may even be indispensable to further progress. The patient is giving himself a breathing space, while he absorbs the discoveries thus far made; he must have an opportunity for consolidating his forces before he is ready to press further. There can be crucial turning points, however, where if he is ever going to take in a deeply buried aspect of his problem he must stand his ground and "grasp the nettle." As we have seen, it takes extensive knowledge of the particular case and considerable skill on the part of the therapist to be sure that such a crisis has been reached; and then the matter calls for delicate handling. Once again, there are no general rules for determining when a plateau has ceased to be a useful period of absorbing insight and begun to threaten the whole analysis with bogging down into immobility. Furthermore, the outer defensive structure varies from one person to the next, and a knowledge of the proper order in which to tackle problems —from the most superficial to the most deeply buried—can greatly expedite matters. A plateau, or signs of resistance and sabotage, may indicate that a particular line of exploration should be abandoned for the time being and a new approach adopted. All attempts to represent the self spatially are apt to be misleading, because spatial diagrams are static while the self incorporates living processes. Nevertheless, if the metaphor is not strained unduly, the neurotic person can be likened to a citadel fortress. If the defenses are impregnable at one gate, it is better to try at another, until gradually so many troops filter in at various entrances that the inmost chamber is surrounded. Then there may be a final, bloody, dangerous battle before the fortress surrenders. Occasionally, however, the beleaguered antagonist, when all paths of escape have been cut off, will accept defeat rather gracefully, sign a truce with great relief, and go out to fraternize with his former enemies.

A period of deepened awareness of conflict, after the first comfort and cleansing of purgation, can be most discouraging, however. In such a period the patient may have no concrete experience, as yet, which provides a basis for realizing and enjoying what it would be like to have a "new," more harmonious self. He stands poised between the only self he has ever had and an unknown future—an abyss into which he must leap, without knowing whether there is any bottom. The "old" self has made him unhappy; but *having* it has, naturally, seemed indispensable to him. The compromises, rationalizations, defenses and illusions which he has built up in the past have at least enabled him to keep going; in fact, they are interwoven with everything he regards as giving him superiority, security and worth. What guarantee does he have that if he loosens his grasp on assets-and-liabilities all at once he will not be deprived of the assets without getting rid of the liabilities? At this point it is important to take into account the fact that many neurotic people give their fantasies the value of reality. The accomplishments they dream about, the change in luck, the wonderful mate they are going to find some day, register not merely as far-off events that will *then* make everything all right, but as present possessions which make the ongoing moments tolerable. To deprive them of such fantasies is not merely to rob them of hope for the future but of morale in the present. "Reality," as contrasted with these fantasies, seems rough and odious. They can derive no exhilaration from grappling with it. They cannot believe that by coming to term with it they may uncover latent strength which will enable them to enjoy it and will give them a much more stable foundation for self-esteem and self-confidence.

In such situations, the troubled person needs some one who believes in him. The therapist does not convey this faith by elaborate reassurances or glowing tales concerning what it is going to be like when the conflicts are resolved. He conveys it rather by working with those capacities in the patient which have already contributed insight and which can carry forward a further exploration of the problem. Naturally the fact that the doctor has seen many others come through tight spots, and the fact that he does not get panicky or discouraged, even when the patient is ready to give up, play a supportive role. Most important of all, however, the patient does not have to face his dilemmas alone—or even with a well-meaning blunderer. He faces them in fellowship with some one in whom he can have confidence, even when he has lost all confidence in himself.

It would be foolish to deny that this faith in the therapist can make a decisive difference at moments when it is nip-and-tuck as to whether the patient will retreat behind old defenses or march forward into the unknown. In such moments, therapists are mediators of the kind of faith in the ultimate meaningfulness of life which is at the core of religion—whether they like this or not. The danger of "playing God" in the lives of people, which certainly must not be minimized, should not blind us to the fact that men can be instruments in the service of healing power. The endowments and skills of the therapist as an individual are immeasurably enhanced by the fact that he is the symbol of something much greater than himself—namely, the drive toward fellowship, wholeness and honesty which is deeply rooted in human life.

Because there are periods when the patient is so heavily dependent, a gradual transition to a position of independence may be difficult to effect. There are clinging-vine types who, provided they are wealthy enough, begin to enjoy psycho-analysis so much that if one therapist finally tosses them out of the nest they will merely look up another one. There is no way of safeguarding psycho-analysis from the reputation it gets from chattery dowagers who "tried it" at some point in a sequence which may also include a chiropractor, the Oxford Group Movement, a "success" school, Rosicrucianism and Christian Science. Furthermore, the transference may cast the therapist in a father-role or a lover-role which puts great demands on his ingenuity. For example, no matter how astutely he may confine himself to following out factual implications, the patient will twist these into a scolding. The latter has come to the interview to be punished; he feels that his guilt will be cancelled by such punishment; and he is thwarted if the paternal whipping is not administered. In order to illustrate the wheels-within-wheels which can be encountered in an analysis, we should add that such self-castigation and desire for punishment may arise from the patient's attempt to prove that he is a very conscientious, remorseful, ethically sensitive person. Yet at a deeper level, he is not really sorry at all; the wallowing in remorse is a convenient way of avoiding a full and frank examination of what prompted him to commit the "sin."

One final requisite on the part of the therapist needs to be mentioned because a fair proportion of his patients are likely to be highly educated. Many such people are estranged from their own feelings because they assume that unless something can be grasped in a neat, clear-cut way it is not worth considering. They find it difficult to catch on to a method which involves verbalizing impulses and reactions "as they come," with little attempt at the outset to discriminate between what is important and what is trivial. They tend to be interested in understanding the theoretical concepts and the technical terminology connected with psycho-analysis. They may even be intrigued by the ways in which these concepts can be applied to themselves and other people—especially to other people, and more especially to parents or mates. But if left to themselves they would make a chess-game of the entire therapeutic relationship. A simple, forthright "registering" of rage, or emptiness, or helplessness (with all "interesting" interpretations side-tracked for the moment) is alien to them, and extremely uninviting. They can talk about their problems at a great rate and with eloquent virtuosity; but they cannot afford to sit still, or lie still—and look—and feel. Often it takes weeks of work before such patients will cease "organizing" their confessions in a 1, 2, 3 manner, and proffering elaborate schematisms to explain what is going on. For understandable reasons, they use their special skill in abstract thinking to keep attention diverted from what they do not want to recognize. If their technical knowledge and their capacity for verbalization are in some respects superior to those of the therapist, they may feel that they understand things better than he does and that he is slow to catch on. Yet if the therapist knows his business, he will not be drawn into a contest to see who can win theoretical arguments.

CHAPTER IV

The Development of Personal Belief

WE NOW TURN, in this and succeeding chapters, to a discussion of the bearing of psychotherapy upon Christian views of man. Subsequently we shall examine specific problems; but first we need a general description of how psychological and cultural influences affect the development of religious belief. This general description is meant to apply primarily to the American scene, but it inevitably reflects circumstances some of which characterize modern civilization pervasively.

The foregoing chapters make it obvious that a belief cannot be understood apart from what it means dynamically to the person who holds it. Not only in religion but in all forms of conviction, the words and ideas by means of which we formulate beliefs may mean radically different things to different people. Consider, for example, belief in democracy. To a Nazi it meant supporting the degenerate plutocracies of the West. To a Russian it may mean government by the people provided that "the people" be equated with "the Party." An Englishman associates democracy quite naturally with constitutional monarchy. The possibility of such an association may not even enter the mind of an American; and among Americans themselves the word connotes incompatible things to a Southern believer in white supremacy, a devotee of the *Chicago Tribune,* a C.I.O. organizer, and a Harvard professor of political science.

The further we move away from abstract, unambiguous notions, such as those employed in pure mathematics, and into areas where thinking is intimately connected with hopes and fears, loves and hates, the more impossible does it become to specify what a word or an idea means apart from the living content which the individual confers upon it. As we have seen, acceptance or rejection of such emotionally charged ideas may be partly, and even mainly, determined by unconscious factors.

Before any of us have reached the point where we can employ objective, critical thinking, a whole set of dynamic attitudes have already established themselves as enhancing or threatening our sense of security. A child who has been brought up by his father to believe that science is the only pathway to truth may react violently the first time he encounters some one who challenges this assumption. He is not old enough to understand the merits of the issue as an intellectual question. He is aware only of the fact that his father's infallibility is being questioned; he has grown up thinking that what his family accepts is right, and ideas which challenge this assumption are not to be weighed or examined, they are threats to be countered. A child brought up in a Fundamentalist home would have similar reactions in connection with an opposite set of beliefs. The same point could be illustrated equally well in connection with the father's political convictions. Our first ventures into thinking about controversial questions are bound to be of such a character that we use our capacities for learning facts and for tying them together into arguments in the service of maintaining our own sense of being in the right and of belonging to a group which is in the right. The ability to think objectively and critically gradually comes on the scene (if it ever does!) with the stage already set. And to the end of our days, our thinking about questions which affect our own interests never can be divorced completely from the way in which emotional patterns have been influenced by parents, community and surrounding culture. Hence the way to truth, where questions of value are involved, lies not in the direction of getting rid of our feelings, but in the direction of becoming as fully aware of them as possible—including those which were hitherto buried in the unconscious.

Religion incorporates our most passionate hopes and fears, our deepest sense of solidarity with other human beings and with cosmic power, our most intimate commitments, and our most crucial beliefs concerning the value of life. Therefore, it is not surprising that in religion the connection between the operative meaning of an idea and the character-structure of the individual should be especially close. This does not mean, as some psychologists and philosophers have claimed, that issues of truth and falsity are irrelevant to religion—unless it follows that such issues are also irrelevant to all questions in economics, politics, ethics and philosophy where personal commitment is involved. But it does mean that if we are concerned to replace invalid beliefs with valid ones, we must be willing to take account of matters which go beyond logical coherence and intellectual precision. Our emotions can *prevent* us from grasping truths which we have the intellectual capacity to understand and accept; but they can also *implement* our search for truth and our willingness to act in the light of it. Where questions of value are involved, the most consistent theory imaginable is impotent unless people believe it with their hearts as well as with their heads.

Let us acknowledge, then, that feelings and unconscious motives, as well as intellectual processes, play a part in the formulation of religious beliefs, and that this is not necessarily to their discredit. Our statement applies just as inescapably to negative as to positive attitudes—as much to the atheist as to the man who believes in God. Hence it is not intended to settle questions of truth and falsity. It is intended, rather, to widen the context in which we approach such questions, and to counteract the illusion that we can afford to regard ourselves as pure thinking machines.

In this connection the discoveries of psychotherapy are relevant to a distinction which has always been important to religion itself, the distinction between genuine faith and pseudo-faith. These discoveries enable us to see more clearly how willingness to accept truth, as contrasted with the inclination to distort or evade it, depends upon inner security as well as intellectual acumen. Most religious traditions call attention to the difference between believing a doctrine only theoretically and believing it whole-heartedly. The former is likely to be sterile;

the latter unites intellectual assent with warm feeling and eager action. The implications of this difference need to be examined thoroughly. For if it be true that beliefs on momentous human issues cannot be held in a purely theoretical way unless a serious estrangement of some sort has taken place within the individual, then several contemporary assumptions should be revised. In scientific and philosophical circles, and in some liberal religious circles, the validity of a belief is thought to be directly proportional to its dispassionateness. This is an error almost as bad as the opposite one of equating intensity of feeling with certainty.

"Objectivity" has become a fetish in the last few centuries through an understandable mistake. Science and rationality do require dispassionateness, and virtually all forms of illusion, superstition and fanaticism are connected with passionate commitment. Thus it is easy to fall into the blunder of regarding dispassionateness as an end in itself, and to become blind to the dehumanizing consequences of the blunder. Actually detachment is commendable only as a means of directing our *attachments* to more valid concepts of the universe and of man's nature and goals. A disjunction between detachment and attachment presents us with a false dilemma. We do not have to choose between cold objectivity and blind feeling. Indeed, failure to establish organic, mutually enriching, connections between reason and emotion is neurotic, and we have seen how the therapist must combine the clarity of the scientist with the sympathy of the father-confessor in trying to deal with neuroses. Our scientific studies of religion and of cultural ideologies have made us thoroughly aware of the perils of illusion and fanaticism. But have they made us adequately aware of the perils of a scientific or philosophical detachment which is not concerned about the human consequences of its findings?

Estrangement between reason and emotion is often connected with the fact that we receive our beliefs at the hands of parents (and the institutions they represent) and the gradual process of being permitted to think and feel for ourselves may be blocked in various ways. Many of us reach maturity with social, moral and religious assumptions which we have either passively accepted or had forced down our throats, instead of having found an opportunity to work them out and verify them for ourselves. When a child's spontaneous reactions are met with ridicule or punishment they are driven underground with the label "silly" or "dangerous" attached. As we have seen, this does not mean that they cease to operate; and if a person's conscious beliefs are sterile and rigid the explanation may be that they have been robbed of the support of his feelings. Such beliefs can even be employed as a strait jacket to keep "dangerous" reactions from expressing themselves.

The foregoing statement does not imply that organized religion inevitably enslaves the growing child while the absence of organized religion fosters the independent development of his own convictions. Most great human concerns are necessarily maintained and propagated by means of institutions. The transition from receiving beliefs to adopting them independently must be made *within* the framework of institutions—home, school and government, as well as religious affiliations or some substitute for them. It is just as possible to reach independence within a religious tradition as to accept monogamy because one sees the value of it instead of because one is frightened into conforming to it automatically. Indeed, no one can be religious, even though his religion may fall outside the confines of the churches, without finding some means of expressing his personal faith within a tradition and a community which implement it. While only a few men can be religious pioneers (prophets), every one can discover the applicability of a belief to his own life. The fact that the belief may be centuries old and commonly accepted among his associates need neither prevent him from making it his own nor compel him to do so.

The difference between genuine faith and pseudo-faith is determined by whether the individual can be "honest" with himself generally, in the sense described in Chapter III. Two questions are involved. First, is what he believes true? Second, is the way he believes it whole-hearted? These questions are closely related in practice, and inner conflicts can prevent a person from reaching beliefs which are true in content. Yet the distinction is important because one can give sincere assent (consciously) to sound, well-established ideas, and still lack enthusiasm for them or violate them involuntarily. Much "hypocrisy" in religion, and in other aspects of life, is due far more to unrecognized and uncontrollable discrepancies between the head and the heart than to any deliberate attempt to be deceitful. Take, for example, a moral philosopher who is thoroughly acquainted with the best text-books on ethical theory. Suppose that he has worked out a consistent, inclusive conception of how interests are related to duty. His definitions of "pleasure," "happiness," "right" and "good" are precise. His propositions concerning their mutual connections are logically impeccable. Nevertheless, because of influences beyond his control, he is an intensely ego-centric, insecure, stuffy, hostile person. Therefore much of the real content of his human relations goes counter to his ethical beliefs, despite the fact that he holds the latter sincerely. His knowledge of "the good" lacks vital connection with the rest of his character structure. And the more egocentric and insecure he is, the more oblivious he becomes to the discrepancy between his fine ethical ideals and his underlying reactions toward people.*

The path to maturity in religion is the same as the path to maturity generally. During childhood, it is natural that we should be dependent upon adults for guidance in matters of behavior and thinking. Granted a pair of healthy parents, the transition from dependence to independence takes place without undue stress and strain. The child is allowed to assume responsibility as he becomes able to shoulder it. Departure from parental standards is not regarded indiscriminately as rebelliousness or waywardness on his part. It is recognized as a possible sign of the

---

*One more example from a nonreligious sphere. I have seen a man get red in the face, roar and pound the table in defense of his belief that dispassionate, scientific objectivity is the only way of getting at the truth—without being conscious in the least of the discrepancy between his actions and his thesis.

unfolding of a distinct personality. Even when the parents are convinced that a line of thought or action goes contrary to the child's real interests as well as theirs, they also realize that, within limits, an opportunity to learn by trial-and-error is indispensable to the development of strength and wisdom.

Unfortunately, however, this optimum pattern is not only violated in general, it is violated in quite special ways with regard to religious training. In large segments of Judaism, Catholicism and Protestantism, if the parents are "firm believers" then religion is the subject concerning which independent, critical thought is *least* encouraged. The child is given no grounds for believing that his religious tradition is something he can gradually make his own; he is expected to swallow it, as it is spooned into him, without asking questions. Often the energies of the parents and the Church are directed toward rooting a docile, unquestioning subservience in the child's make-up so firmly that his faith will stay with him when he confronts the doubts and temptations of the world. This authoritarian approach ignores the fact that the most effective way to deal with the doubts and temptations of later life is to begin as early as possible in nurturing those capacities for independent judgment, critical thought and spiritual discernment which enable a person to cope with unforeseeable circumstances as they arise.

Two opposite pathways are open to a child who grows up under such conditions. First, he may remain docile and subservient, and so long as he can avoid situations that compel him to question his inherited beliefs, he may get along indefinitely without much trouble. Clearly, however, he is in a vulnerable position. His religion is largely a matter of habit, an unthinking bit of filial piety. Ordinarily he does not reflect about it at all; but occasionally he wonders why there is so little connection between it and his everyday life. He derives no genuine strength from his faith, and when a crisis arises either he finds that faith empty or he clings to it blindly as a means of escaping the full impact of peril, misery, sickness or grief.

In the second place, the child may rebel. The rebellion can

take the form of open conflict with his parents, and it can include virtually everything. He rebels in connection with the choice of a school, a job, a mate, politics, and moral standards, as well as religion. Frequently, however, an especially deep-seated revulsion for the Church is instilled in adolescents because it is pervasively associated with oppressive restrictions. It connotes being "good," and the sort of goodness in question may reflect rigidity and other uninviting traits in his elders. The child gets the notion that morality and religion are strait jackets woven by adults. The more vitality he has, the more he seeks ways of combating them. Thus he is excluded from learning that his own welfare is based upon what is valid in morality and religion. His energy is concentrated upon resisting his parents' standards and does not get directed toward developing positive standards of his own. The worst tragedies of adolescence, including juvenile delinquency, are partly traceable to the fact that vitality, joy in living, longing for adventure, and maturing sexual desire *can* only express themselves, in many homes and community environments, through the negative pathway of rebellion.

Often, of course, the revolt is covert instead of open. The child avoids a fight, pretends to knuckle under, and then breaks loose as soon as he can get away from parental or school authorities. Such disobedience is accompanied by an exhilarating sense of freedom or painful feelings of guilt or both; usually both. In any case it has the undesirable result of making the child deceitful; and it deprives him of what ought to be his best sources of adult guidance and understanding.

In sharp contrast with the authoritarian imposition of religion, we are increasingly confronted with the opposite sort of phenomenon. The child is given no religious instruction whatever. It is banned from the public schools; and at home the parents conduct their lives on the basis, say, of sexual promiscuity, plenty of liquor, and an exploitative, materialistic philosophy. One might well ask: "If you don't like the authoritarian structure of the old-fashioned, religiously conservative home, do you propose to offer this 'modern' home as a suitable substitute?" The answer, of course, is that neither is a remedy for the other. Steady, dependable affection between the parents, and a home-life based on stable, genuinely affirmed moral principles, are necessary if a child is to have the sense of security he needs. Moreover, the fact that he may be free from religious and moralistic restrictions does not mean, in such a home as the one just described, that he is really free from being exploited and dominated. He may be caught in an emotional tug-of-war between the parents. He may be packed off to a private school as early as possible, and to summer camps as often as possible. He may be criticized and rejected if he does not fulfill the requirements of charm, cleverness and precocious sophistication which are prized in the parents' social set. He may be left free to believe anything he wants on "spiritual" matters, but howled at with disdain if he utters any doubts, with the first burgeonings of intelligence, about the capitalistic system and the Republican party. He may even be looked upon as "queer" if he so much as shows interest in religion.

I do not mean to suggest that all "unreligious" homes are immoral and unstable. But parents who are alienated from the Church, or for whom Church membership is a trivial matter, often take pride in the fact that they leave their children free to make up their own minds on religious questions. This might seem to be exactly what I am recommending; but it is not. For in such homes the children are left free concerning whatever the parents regard as unimportant, but steadily indoctrinated concerning whatever they take seriously. To bring children up with the impression that religion is a side-issue is not really broadminded and tolerant at all. Even though the parents (perhaps without trying very hard) have found no Church which meets their own religious needs, this does not mean that religion is a side-issue with them, either. It means rather that they direct their capacities for devotion into other channels—money, power, sex, nationalism, clubs, causes and "culture." So long as they lack a stable philosophy of life, an integrating center for their loyalties, and a deep sense of solidarity with their fellows, their existence is bound to be scattered and unsatisfying even though they do not take time to recognize the fact.

Against these extremes of rigid authoritarianism and spiritual rootlessness which can be found in American family life, we should recognize that a child needs to grow up in an atmosphere where the behavior and inner content of his parents' lives are basically consistent with the ethical and religious principles they acknowledge. He should be permitted to formulate his own beliefs, within this context, as rapidly as his capacities for independent thought, moral judgment and religious decision mature. When the parents possess warmth, integrity and effective ideals, it is natural and desirable for their children to emulate them far more than they break away from them. Yet even in an ideal family situation, the role of emotional factors remains primary and the role of intellectual instruction derivative. The child's foremost need is an adequate supply of wise love. By "wise" I mean steady and natural, instead of sporadic and forced; unsentimental and geared to growing autonomy, instead of plaintive and smothering. If this need is met, he does not have to be indoctrinated with the propositions that love is fundamental in ethics and religion, and that human life is precious and deserving of respect. As he encounters such propositions he will recognize that they express intellectually what he has already experienced. On the other hand, if such affection is lacking no amount of indoctrination concerning the exalted or obligatory character of love can fill the vacuum.

Where there is a sharp discrepancy in the home between inner attitudes and professed standards, a deep sense of hopelessness and personal worthlessness can easily get established in the child; and the higher the professed ideals, the more intense his sense of failure becomes. Out of such a situation two opposite types of reaction grow. First, a clinging to ideals and religious convictions in an attempt to assure oneself that the universe is a secure place and that life is worth-while—*despite* the unsatisfactoriness of actual experience. This is the familiar phenomenon where religion is used as an escape mechanism. Second, a cynical rejection of ideals and religious beliefs as "bunk" because of the discrepancy between what they enshrine and what the individual has actually encountered in life.

Where the parents' ethical and religious ideas are basically in line with a mature capacity to give and to receive love, the child has an opportunity to grow into convictions which are integral with his own reactions to life. In other words, wherever healthy conditions surround their development, children will grow into religion of the "once born" variety. Their conversion will be a matter of gradual, natural appropriation of workable beliefs, instead of a shattering experience of being torn asunder and reassembled on a new basis. The fact that much religion has been of the "twice born" variety, where serenity and beatitude are reached only after severe conflict, indicates both that the conditions surrounding human growth have often been unhealthy, and that religion has had to make its way against this unhealthiness.

Our discussion thus far has suggested that religious conviction can be genuine only insofar as what one affirms doctrinally is an attempt to give intellectual expression to personal relationships and vital experience. Many theologians would want to protest at this point that a doctrine can be true even though a given individual has not reached a position where he can apprehend its truth; moreover, discrepancies between one's intellectual beliefs and his practices may be due to lack of maturity and discipline rather than to any defect in the propositions he accepts with his mind.

Let us examine these protests. It is certainly true that there can be riches in a doctrinal tradition which go far beyond the individual's experience and which are nevertheless of great value to others and potentially of great value to him. In many areas besides religion we cannot wait upon a spontaneous acceptance which may never be forthcoming. In the transmission of scientific knowledge, legal standards and æsthetic taste we do not regard the private judgment and limited experience of one individual as the final court of appeal. On the contrary, we take for granted a collective heritage which has been built up and maintained by institutions and groups. We assume that the educational task consists largely in enabling a person to appreciate and absorb what this heritage makes available. His adequacy is determined by how he fits into the best that civilization has to offer; the validity of scientific theories, legal principles and artistic canons is by no means to be judged by whether they fit his personal predilections. Hence it may also be contended that in religion the authority of the tradition or the institution is paramount; insight and maturity are reached not by having each individual "cook up" his own ideas, but by training each generation in the appropriation of a collective wisdom.

Such a line of argument incorporates undeniable and important truths. But the crucial question does not turn upon the presence or the absence of an authoritative tradition in any of these spheres. The crucial question arises in connection with the spirit and goal of that educational process which the tradition is designed to serve and to carry forward. Is subservience to the tradition regarded as an end in itself? Or is passive dependence upon it regarded as, at best, a transitional stage whereby the individual is exposed to conserved values of the past in order that he may employ them fully in fashioning his own life in the ongoing present?

The usual argument in defense of the former alternative holds that although it is desirable to have the individual grow as far as possible in understanding what he initially accepts on authority, there are some matters where most men or all men lack the competence to comprehend the authoritative doctrine. In connection with such matters, private judgment must be made subordinate to what the tradition or the Church teaches. Otherwise the result is rampant individualism and spiritual anarchy. Religious bodies which hold to this theory of authority can point with considerable effect to the divisiveness of Protestantism and to the chaotic ethical relativism of modern culture in support of their case.

Yet no institution or tradition can be maintained except

through the assent of individuals, one at a time; the only question is the extent to which this assent is free or constrained. Even Roman Catholicism recognizes that each individual must make the basic decision concerning acceptance or rejection of its authority; but it specifies that once the decision is made affirmatively the believer is under obligation to accept unquestioningly whatever the Church teaches as essential, and to confine his critical and independent thinking to areas where the Church has not reached a closed verdict. Obviously the same question concerning the freedom or constraint of assent can be raised in connection with Protestantism. Allegiance can be transferred from an infallible Pope to an infallible Book without abandoning the theory of religious authority outlined above. And even the liberal theology of a creedless branch of Protestantism can be so taught that any child growing up in it comes to regard it solely as a deposit external to him.

Yet there is no escape from the fact that the individual's character-structure both determines and is determined by the functioning of a religious tradition within him. Even though a person may sincerely accept the "whole" tradition on the authority of the Church, certain aspects of it will mean more to him than others. When he encounters aspects with which some of his other thoughts and feelings are irreconcilable, he must either remain blind to the true import of the tradition, or he must regard the other thoughts and feelings as wrong, or he must unconsciously resist these aspects of the tradition even though he feels under obligation to accept them.

Since the obstacles to ethical and religious insight are not merely intellectual, but include those emotional conflicts which prevent a person from living the truth that he sees, they can be removed only by a dynamic transformation of the whole self and its center of motivation. Where these obstacles are not serious, the transformation can be a gradual, relatively painless transition from childishness to religious maturity. Where they are serious we encounter the dramatic and sudden *volte face* of the "twice born" conversion. And there are many intermediate degrees between these two extremes. Virtually all branches of Christianity recognize, in theory, that such reorientation of the self cannot be brought about merely through the transmission of doctrine. They recognize that what is most central and precious in faith is an uncoerced alignment of human life with creative and redemptive power. Since the alignment involves a relationship in which the self is only one term, it is not exclusively at the disposal of the individual's will. It occurs only through a coincidence between God's will and man's. Yet the fruits of such faith become, in a real sense, a human possession, and take the form of abiding, dependable attitudes. Faith can continue in a man only as it is replenished at the divine source; yet it is genuinely his. The personal orientation in which faith consists is acknowledged to be the only authentic basis for belief. Acceptance of doctrine can be vital and whole-hearted only when it is an attempt to formulate in words and concepts something which actually happens within the life of the man.

The practice of the Christian Churches, however, has often been at odds with what is thus acknowledged in theory. Even when doctrine is explicitly regarded as derivative from the experience of conversion and from continuing fellowship with God, it has nevertheless been employed as a norm for evaluating the genuineness and depth of such experience and fellowship. At the worst, the Churches have acted as though Christianity could be transmitted by getting people to say "yes" to dogmas. But even at best, the primary aim of Christian education and evangelism has been to evoke religious experiences and conversions which fit into accepted conceptions of God and Christ, instead of to uncover at the outset *whatever is going on* at the deepest, most immediate, and most genuine level. A discovery of "whatever is going on" might compel a teacher or pastor to conclude that the individual concerned was extremely immature and spiritually impoverished. Yet the underlying immaturity and poverty can never be brought to light and remedied so long as approved phrases are used by children and adults as a sanctimonious "cover up," or recited by rote because such phrases are known to be what is expected in Sunday School and Church. Many pastors are continually amazed that people who have been brought up in Christian homes and who have attended church all their lives are not more deeply affected by the teachings they say they accept. If hidden and unconscious factors were brought into the picture, the discrepancy between Christian teaching and "how people really run their lives" would be even more startling. Yet in most church circles it is regarded as dangerous to suggest that one of the reasons for the ineffectuality of organized religion (insofar as it is ineffectual) lies in the fact that "what one ought to believe" (or *must* believe if he is to be a real Christian) is given priority over the question "what do I actually believe—as indicated by my actions, my attitudes toward people, my spontaneous attractions and repulsions?"

Insofar as the central convictions of Christianity concerning God, Christ, the Bible, the sacraments and the fellowship of believers have lost their life-transforming persuasiveness, the fault does not lie wholly with the perversity and secularism of the modern world. Sometimes the fault lies also in the fact that men have not been given an opportunity to discover at first-hand the healing power which these convictions represent. This comment does not apply solely to rigidly authoritarian versions of the Christian faith. Liberal theology also focuses attention upon "what should I believe?" instead of upon "what do I believe?" (in the sense just described). It merely offers content different from conservative theology in answering the "should"—content which is more enlightened, and more anæmic.

These considerations have a direct bearing upon the difference between a defensive and a secure religious orientation. If a person is basically insecure that fact is bound to be reflected in the way he holds *any* beliefs, although the specific content of his beliefs can aggravate the problem. Here are some of the reasons an insecure person may have for wanting to be able to count on the rightness of the doctrines, rituals and requirements of his Church: Orthodoxy may give him a sense of superior righteousness; belonging to the "true" Church, with valid orders and sacraments, can give him a position of advantage over pagans and members of heretical Churches; religious ideals and requirements can be used to hold down unacceptable impulses which would otherwise break into the open. Under such circumstances a person needs to find ways of making his faith impregnable against criticism coming from others or from skeptical inclinations within himself. These defensive attitudes can take on countless ramifications; but one general rule applies to them. The more estranged the individual is from reality (and his estrangement may be partly due to following vulnerable beliefs), the more he is compelled to bolster his defensive structure.

Man's capacities for imagination and for logical thinking can be employed to construct a system which *excludes* evidence from the world outside and doubts from within. When such a system derives its cohesiveness from the need of an insecure person to hold himself together and to reassure himself that the universe meets his specifications, it is bound to be employed in "filtering" or "retouching" reality, and there is no effective way of refuting it by means of logical argument. For one thing, an examination of the various strands woven into the system may disclose that it is tightly coherent. But even where discrepancies and inconsistencies can be pointed out, the human mind possesses endless ingenuity for getting around such inconveniences when it needs to. The "believer," when challenged, may retort that his views, like life, are deeper than logic. (And life *is* deeper than logic.) Or he may insist that the inconsistencies and uncertainties affect only peripheral matters, while what is essential remains untouched. Or he may point out that every attempt to formulate a world-view in words is unsatisfactory, but that his is less so than any alternative. Insofar as he is compelled, for the sake of (pseudo)security, to place his system as a cushion between himself and reality, the only effective remedy is to create an atmosphere where it is safe for him to employ those buried or repudiated resources in himself which could lead to a revision and expansion of his awareness. If such factors are literally non-existent or inaccessible, the man is psychotic; and the dividing line between a rigid dogmatism and a completely delusional system is sometimes extremely difficult to draw. Any one who has worked in a mental hospital knows that many of its patients live in private worlds which are only slightly more bizarre than those of people who are walking the streets outside and occupying positions of prominence and power in public life. We have confined this discussion to the way in which theological systems can be functionally related to insecurity, because an understanding of religious development (both benign and malignant) is our primary concern in this chapter. But the same psychological considerations apply to other kinds of systems. For example, paranoids who are still well-oriented enough to run large businesses can usually find a Congressional committee that will take their political ideas seriously.

For the most part the Churches have not yet learned that the best way to pass from defensive rationalizations to secure faith is to let doubts, inconsistencies, confusions and rebellions come out into the open instead of using various forms of spiritual coercion to keep them hidden or to drive them from awareness altogether. More will be said presently concerning secure faith, but it should already be clear that such faith rests upon an integration between rational belief and emotional commitment. We should acknowledge, however, that the Church's deficiencies at this point have been no more startling than the deficiencies of our educational system. In the latter case we have assumed that by training people in the use of empirical evidence and consistent reasoning we can equip them to understand how reality works and to cope with it, as adequately as possible, in the service of humane ends. But anxiety, hostility and emotional conflict cannot be removed by the means to which this assumption has attached primary importance. Appeals to "science and reason" (as ordinarily understood) cannot remove basic blockages to sound interpersonal relationships and moral insight; and even our best academic institutions have made little more than a dent on the problem posed by students whose knowledge may be adequate in a chosen field, but who are foredoomed to personal unhappiness and impaired social usefulness because of unresolved emotional problems. If we went further afield and considered the slowness with which psychiatric knowledge has been brought to bear upon the need for a wholesale overhauling of our penal system, the resulting indictment would have to be even more severe.

The last remarks are not offered in order to excuse the Church; but its limitations should be viewed in the light of the culture in which it finds itself. On its man-ward side the Church can be no better than the people who belong to it. And the adverse psychological conditions in which they, and their culture, and their Churches have been caught were not well understood until recently. Perhaps it would be more accurate to say that many of these adverse conditions are very imperfectly understood even today.

Because the distinction between faith and reason can be employed in a defensive fashion, and often has been so employed, many scientists and philosophers have leaped to the conclusion that the only way to safeguard against special pleading on behalf of a religious doctrine or tradition is to abandon faith entirely, and to regard reason as the sole source of truth in religious matters as in all others. This is a mistake. The term "faith," when properly understood, expresses a meaning which is indispensable to religion. This meaning is *sui generis;* it cannot be reduced to or analyzed into other terms without loss. Indeed, a retention and clarification of the concept provides one of the indispensable bases for differentiating between religion and other concerns.

Let us agree, for the sake of the argument, that if a question can be settled by means of scientific evidence, historical research or philosophical reflection, it should not be settled by faith. What remains? Many will say that the only questions which remain are in principle unanswerable because we can never hope to have verifiable knowledge in connection with them. Yet it does not follow that since we cannot operate on the basis of verifiable knowledge we therefore remain practically neutral in relation to

such questions. On the contrary, our basic orientations of trust
or despair toward the meaning of life will go beyond knowledge,
no matter what attitude we adopt. Take a naturalistic humanist
as a test case. He is sure that his own life and the lives of his
fellows incorporate specific values (and disvalues) here and now.
He is sure that through the fulfillment of natural conditions he
can conserve or increase the availability of human satisfactions
in the future. He asserts that this is all we can know, and that
a desire or an effort to know more about the significance of
life than what it actually incorporates or fails to incorporate
in the ongoing temporal process, is both futile and infantile. And
so long as he concentrates on the word "know," he may be
right. Nevertheless, such a thinker's underlying assumptions about
the status of values are arrived at by means of a commitment
which goes beyond demonstrable knowledge; and this commitment carries with it definite implications concerning the limits
within which human life must reach such worth and meaning
as it can possess. It is arrived at by presuppositions of the same
order as those involved in religious faith. Even if one declares
that attempts to formulate an over-all view on such matters are
fruitless, the declaration itself rests upon an "over-all" view.

Therefore, it would be helpful if we could reserve the word
"faith" for the responses a man makes to ultimate questions
which *in principle* cannot be answered by means of knowledge.
Frequently discussions of both faith and "religious knowledge"
sound as though God were one entity among others, distinct from
the world and man. Belief then takes the form of affirming that
this entity exists, and unbelief takes the form of denying that it
does. This manner of stating the issue obscures the fact that
religion essentially is an acceptance of life as grounded in whatever evokes unreserved devotion; it is characterized by a sense
of internal harmony, and of oneness with nature, humanity and
"the ground of being." As John Dewey has pointed out in *A
Common Faith,* this religious attitude is often found, in contemporary society, among people who do not profess to believe
in God and who direct their devotion to "secular" goals. Much

confusion could be removed in both theology and philosophy if we could recognize that conceptions of God are attempts to characterize the ultimate context in which natural and human events take place; and that other characterizations of the object or objects of religious devotion are competing attempts of the same order. So long as theologians persist in talking about the "supernatural" as though it were a second world, either hermetically sealed off from or interacting with the world in which human beings exist, naturalists and humanists are entirely right in replying that they prefer to confine their interests to the one world which we indubitably have on our hands. Unless attention is fixed upon the relationship between the object* of religious concern (however conceived) and the meaning of human life (its possibilities and limits), the ensuing debate can wander endlessly at cross-purposes, without ever bringing to light the venture of faith which underlies the naturalistic or humanistic position. Moreover, if this same definition of faith could be accepted, many religious tenets which are now retained as "articles of faith" might be seen to belong properly to those areas where scientific evidence, historical research and philosophical reflection are equipped to furnish dependable answers.

So long as we regard human beings as divided into two groups —those who follow "faith" versus those who follow "reason"— the issues are being wrongly conceived. "Faith" and "reason" are names for two different capacities which can operate in any man; insofar as they are at odds with each other, the man is at odds with himself. The attempt to settle anything by an appeal to faith which can be clarified or tested by means of reason is obscurantist; but the attempt to ignore or to eradicate everything that cannot be settled by reason involves stifling the most potent source of creativity and transformation in human life. In other words, what goes into extra-rational commitment in the face of momentous ethical and religious decisions becomes a

*I use the word "object" here in a neutral sense to denote what religious concern is directed toward. This usage does not exclude and is not incompatible with the belief that God is a "Subject."

dangerous source of illusion and fanaticism when it is estranged from reason; but reason, if it attempts to remain "pure" by withdrawing from passionate commitment and trust, becomes arid, theoretical and impotent.

At the center of vital religion stands the awareness that reality is wider and richer than any conceptual system we can build in attempting to grasp it. Even more important is the discovery, in personal experience, that some aspects of reality and some ways of coming to terms with existence which have been excluded from conscious thinking are healing, life-giving and transforming. When powers are unleashed which put an end to conflict and enable a person to achieve wholeness and internal harmony on a new level, religion speaks of those powers as coming from "beyond" the individual's own thought and will—and the religious description is quite accurate. What has released the individual from his previous bondage to conflict is not some propositional truth which he has learned, not some new information about the universe which he has acquired, not some theory (whether theistic or otherwise) to which he has given intellectual assent. In a sense, he wakes up to the same world and the same self; yet both have been overwhelmingly transformed, not through something he has consciously willed, but—usually—through something which has worked through him despite himself.

Insofar as this realignment turns out to be deep and stable, the person concerned will quite naturally want to find rational means of testing and interpreting it. He will not feel the need to protect his experience against rational criticism; for insofar as it is genuine, it cannot be undermined, and no amount of "thinking" could possibly take it away from him. Tensions between faith and reason may indeed remain within him, because of the fact that all attempts to formulate the inner transformation in intellectual terms are abstract as compared with the concrete event itself. But his basic disposition will be toward resolving these tensions so far as possible, instead of regarding conflict between faith and reason as something desirable, or as something which vindicates the profundity of the former. He will find that intellectual processes, when carried on within a widened self-acquaintance and an unfrightened openness to whatever experience may bring, can lead him into the exploration of areas that his former rigidity excluded. When thought is carried forward in organic relationship with the richness, sensitivity and vitality of first-hand experience, one is content to wait for consistency to emerge instead of trying to force it prematurely upon his data. Security attends the willingness to put into words and ideas (so far as possible) whatever is encountered, and one welcomes the improvement or correction of his attempts to express and interpret his faith intellectually. Knowing as he does the gap between first-hand experience and communicable articulation of it, he gives other men credit for feeling and apprehending more than they can convey; he is more interested in trying to penetrate through the resulting ambiguities and disagreements than in scoring quick dialectical victories over opponents. On the other hand, the effort to maintain consistency by excluding vitality usually springs from a compulsive need to "see" only what one can pigeon-hole and control logically, and to protect oneself against possible refutation.

Another tension between faith and reason, which even the best efforts may only partially resolve, arises from the fact that the basic shift from conflict to integration carries with it and fosters awareness of the criterion by means of which the value of the shift itself is estimated and appreciated. As we saw earlier, prior to the actual experience of that satisfaction which comes with the resolution of conflict, a neurotic individual may be in no position to appreciate the value in question. He may regard his way of looking at things as "normal," and as reflecting the only possible way in which his life can be conducted. Even if he is aware of unhappiness and, in reaction against it, formulates a vision of what would constitute beatitude, the latter is bound to be distorted by his neurotic needs. His picture of beatitude will incorporate elements which only a sick person could enjoy.

The religious claim that revelation is self-authenticating springs from an analogous situation. Reason, though it can be used to explicate or elaborate the first-hand "awakening," cannot of itself bring about the event or supply the criterion by which the value of revelation is appreciated. *What one is awakened to* constitutes that criterion, and all discursive examinations of its worth, in order to be relevant, must issue from a receipt of its worth. One way of expressing this claim is to say: *Credo ut intelligam.* Faith can be confirmed and interpreted by reason operative in a "converted" person, but cannot be adequately tested by reason-in-general, in abstraction from the question of conversion. Another way of expressing the same claim is to say that faith authenticates itself in religious experience, but not in "experience" in general.

Obviously these claims can be used for defensive instead of open purposes. But before concluding that they are always irrational and arbitrary, we should consider the intrinsic difference between religious faith and natural science. In the case of propositions growing out of scientific experiment, an appeal to public verifiability is quite properly invoked; this appeal means that any one who has such training and intelligence as to be able to understand the operational procedures involved and to discriminate between the relevant and the irrelevant can confirm the truth of the proposition for himself. In other words, any mind can reach scientific truth provided that it can fulfill the requisite conditions. Thus even empirical science does not rest upon an appeal to "reason" and "experience" *sans phrase*. It rests upon an appeal to observational alertness carried on within the context of familiarity with a body of previously learned laws and theories.

It should not surprise us that the conditions which have to be fulfilled in reaching religious insight are more complex, and more easily missed; for in this case even the highest degree of observational alertness to sensory data, and the most painstaking care in safeguarding the logical consistency of one's thinking, cannot guarantee a successful outcome. Here the possibility of illusion and error arises in a situation where all the relevant facts may be consciously known, but their living significance is missed or evaded. Here the problem is not: "What is wrong with my perceptual or conceptual equipment?" but "What within the self resists a fundamental change of heart?" Dynamic strategies are involved, and one can understand "error" only as serving a psychologically important function. The individual will not be able to see through and relinquish his "error" except by means of a realignment of his personality such that he can live the truth which he formerly neglected or shunned.

In the past, most philosophical theories of knowledge have been limited in their attempts to explain these blockages which arise from the total character-structure. They have dealt with them in the course of discussing relations between reason and will, but the latter has been conceived of primarily in conscious terms. Notable exceptions have occurred, of course; for example, Pascal's views of faith and reason, and Spinoza's views of emotion and intellect. More recently Schopenhauer, Nietzsche, Kierkegaard and Bergson have, in different ways, discerned the problem. Pragmatism and instrumentalism have also thrown light upon it, though subject to the limitation that if a person's character-structure is defective his evaluation of "results" will be defective too.

Psychotherapists are intimately acquainted with the manner in which attempts to maintain a narrowly organized *ego* can shut "reality" out or distort it. But thus far their energies have been devoted mainly, so far as religion is concerned, to getting rid of illusions instead of to examining *what* one takes in by means of faith.* In the field of human relationships they have investigated the changes in motivation and feeling which must take place before a shift from estrangement to trust can occur. There are always dimensions in the life of another person which I can come to "know" only when he is willing to disclose them and I am sufficiently *en rapport* with him to appreciate the import

---

*Jung and Kunkel are among those who do pay attention to the latter problem. In this same connection, Dr. Harry M. Tiebout has written two interesting psychiatric papers on "Conversion" and "Surrender." In his chapter on "Faith," in *Man for Himself,* Erich Fromm offers a constructive statement from a humanistic standpoint.

of what he discloses. But psychotherapists have largely been prevented from following these clues, derived from the nature of human relationships, into the area of relationships with God. The habit of concentrating upon the psychological meaning of language which expresses an "I—Thou" relationship easily passes over into the illegitimate assumption that such language possesses *only* a psychological meaning.

Often the profoundest form of faith comes to a man only when, despite the fact that he has given up on himself, "something" does not give up on him. Positive faith has not been reached so long as despair predominates; but, in our age especially, many of us cannot find a faith that will stand up except by passing through despair and receiving a stable orientation toward life—cleansed of illusions and defensiveness—on the other side. When that happens the work of healing power (grace) which bestows beatitude as a gift (though not without participation on our part), has a compelling and inescapable quality that is utterly different from the "You *must* believe" of authoritarian threats. In the latter case the individual finds himself under the pressure of demands which override his freedom; in the former case, he finds himself captured by a healing power which enhances his freedom.

No ordinary means of external observation can enable us to differentiate between these two "musts"; and even in the intimacy of psychological or religious counseling it is often impossible to be sure that the two opposed attitudes toward God have been completely disentangled from one another. A useful test, however, is provided in connection with the role of doubt. As many writers have pointed out, doubt itself can reflect either security or insecurity. As an instrument of security, "constructive" doubt is one of man's most powerful and priceless resources in dispelling illusions and breaking spiritual shackles. It rests upon the virtue of intellectual integrity, and it springs from confidence that truth can be reached, or at least that significant progress can be made toward reaching it.

On the other hand, "destructive" doubt is an instrument of

insecurity. Let us glance at a few of its various manifestations. (1) It can be used with great analytical virtuosity to avoid grasping truths which it would be inconvenient for us to see—especially truths which must be grasped as organic wholes, or not at all. (2) It can indicate a perfectionist unwillingness to participate in the rough-and-tumble of life as it comes; thus it provides the aloof individual with a citadel of suspended judgment which shuts him off from having to do what he can with such partial understanding as he may possess at the moment. This type of skepticism is really a lust for superhuman certainty in disguise; it is an all-or-nothing attitude, where if one cannot reach absolute knowledge, he will strive to undermine and deprecate such partial knowledge as is accessible. (3) It can reflect serious conflict and confusion within the personality as a whole, as, for example, in the individual who never quite knows what to think, and who wanders from one position to the next. This may take opposite forms in different people. On the one hand, there is the person who has no convictions of his own because he is so compliant that he agrees involuntarily with whomever he happens to be talking to. On the other hand, there is the person who *also* has no convictions of his own because he cannot think at all except by means of antagonism; until some one expresses an opinion, his mind is a blank, but as soon as a conviction is asserted, he can tear it to pieces, no matter what it is.

Now, in terms of our test, what will be the difference between an appeal to faith which is calculated to avoid and silence criticism, and one which is an attempt to call attention to the fact that the initiating and sustaining power which makes for human beatitude comes from beyond the self? So far as constructive doubt is concerned, the former appeal will regard it as a foe, and the latter will regard it as an ally. There will also be a difference in connection with destructive doubt. Defensive appeals to faith will note its destructiveness, and will construe that destructiveness as confirming the necessity of a dogmatic authoritarianism. Open appeals to faith will assume that the only remedy for destructive doubt (if one is available at all) is to let it blow itself out. Most attempts to remove such doubt by furnishing the "dubious" individual with "the answer" will be regarded as misguided. This does not mean that a religious believer has no right to state his own honest convictions, when they are asked for; nor does it mean that he must refrain from defending them when they are attacked. It means rather than the believer will recognize the inadequacy of any procedure which prevents an individual from discovering as fully as possible the internal situation in which he actually finds himself. At best, only a provisional and temporary value can be attached to helping a person "hold onto something against his doubts" during an emergency.

A great deal of doubt can be turned from a destructive to a constructive employment when attention is focused upon helping a man to take responsibility for his own beliefs. Often his doubt has arisen as a necessary means of resisting pressure from others or of gaining their approval, and he has become so mired in a pattern of defiance-compliance that he has had little opportunity to become aware of what he believes without reference to what so-and-so will think. Once the way is cleared for a person to accept his own likes and dislikes, his own certainties and disillusionments, it is amazing how frequently the man who "didn't believe anything," or "didn't know what he believed," develops consistency and stability as he grows into his own style of life. At its most striking, this process is one in which aloofness, paralysis and cynical disenchantment disappear entirely, to be replaced by convictions and personal relationships for which the individual is literally willing to lay down his life.

From the standpoint of an open appeal to faith, the genuineness of an integral style and philosophy of life outweighs differences of doctrinal formulation. Therefore, it is important to acknowledge that many of the moral and religious values which are contained in Christianity can be affirmed from within a naturalistic perspective. The Christian believer will hold that the effectual operation of love in human life is ultimately due to the nature and activity of God Himself. With regard to transitions from conflict to serenity, from despair to firmness, and from destructive doubt to openness, he will hold that although such transitions involve something which men do themselves, they at the same time put them in touch with, and are carried through in alignment with, God's saving power. But he will regard it as an implicate of his conception of God that men shall make their way to freedom and responsibility through learning how to come to terms with life for themselves; and he will further believe, as an implicate of this conception of God, that the Deity can work through men in ways which go beyond anything we can provide for or confine within our theological or philosophical systems.

One corollary of the attitude here adopted is that it seeks for constructive alliances between the Church and secularism wherever possible. But I am anxious not to underestimate the difficulties which stand in the way of such alliances. One of the most influential "schools" in contemporary Protestant theology takes for granted a sharp conflict between the two, because it takes for granted a sharp antagonism between God and man. Hence it is in a position to warn the Church against compromising with the world, and to condemn the political, economic and social patterns of our civilization because they fall short of the will of God. In Europe especially, this type of theological thinking has exhibited great firmness in the face of persecution and despair. Under circumstances where not only organized religion, but all standards of justice and respect for personality are threatened with destruction, it is not surprising that churchmen should become more interested in consolidating the forces of those who can unite doctrinally and practically in a common allegiance to Christ, than in keeping the "Welcome mat" outside the door for free-thinkers. Therefore, we should not be hasty in criticizing a "defensive" appeal to revelation when it offers solidarity and fellowship in a Church which knows where it stands—against such staggering threats. Nevertheless, because of its predominantly eschatological outlook, this theology has been weak at the point where the Church should be the organizing and regenerative center for earthly human society and culture.

There is no magic formula in religion, any more than in politics and economics, for steering a middle course between chaotic individualism and totalitarian authority. So far as the Church is concerned the latter peril arises whenever it tries to separate itself, in an exclusivist manner, from the world; but the former peril lays it open to capitulation before the so-called "realistic" principles of secularism, and to forgetfulness of its own distinctive message and function. In our country, however, the major line of division is not between Church members and non-members. This may reflect lack of resoluteness on the part of the Church far more than it reflects any deep-seated Christianization of our culture. Nevertheless, one finds people both inside and outside the Church who share substantially the same humanitarian aims; and they are ranged against ominous forces of repression, hatred, and regimentation that are at work in both the Church and the world. It is regrettable that so many who possess discerning compassion for human suffering, æsthetic creativity, selfless devotion to social justice, and fearless loyalty to truth remain outside the Church because they feel that the atmosphere within would stifle them. It is even more regrettable that an inbred contempt for organized religion blinds them to the Church's actual accomplishments (notably in the Ecumenical Movement), and to the relevance of a revived theology to the problems we all confront. Failure to find membership in a religious community leaves them at the mercy of moral relativism and cultural ideologies. In our age, many who have become refugees from organized religion, for the sake of retaining their own freedom and integrity, have discovered that the "secular" havens to which they have fled are far more enslaving. But it still behooves the Church to offer them a fellowship, if it can, which does not enslave at all.

CHAPTER V

The Image of God

THE CHRISTIAN DOCTRINE that man is created in the image of God means two things. First, that, like the rest of nature, man is dependent upon God for coming into existence and for the maintenance of existence. Second, that he possesses unique capacities which distinguish him from the rest of nature.

The form in which this doctrine has been taught in traditional theology implies the notion that there was once a time in history when Adam enjoyed the harmonious, innocent exercise of his human powers, was ruler over the beasts, and possessed direct, intuitive knowledge of God. Then, with some assistance from Eve and the Serpent, he "fell," and the divine image—his original nature—was impaired. Roman Catholicism and orthodox Protestantism have differed in their interpretations at this point. According to the former, Adam had the advantage at the outset, not merely of a perfectly functioning human nature, but also of a special gift from God. When he fell, he lost this gift, and though he retained his human nature it was seriously weakened by the absence of this previous support. According to the most stringent forms of Protestant doctrine, however, what Adam lost in the fall was his proper human nature. This "total corruption" of the image of God has not prevented men from being able to exercise their intelligence in connection with cultural pursuits. Nevertheless, it has meant that since the dawn of history the whole human race has been, in a sense, insane. Individuals have differed significantly both intellectually and ethically, and some have been able to perform deeds that were outstandingly brilliant or good. But all men are egocentric at the core. The proper law of human nature is that it shall fulfill itself through dependence upon and harmony with the will of God. But the law of man's *fallen* nature is that he shall strive to make himself the center of the universe. Since he is unsuited to be that, he suffers from the strife and insecurity which attend his efforts to carry through an impossible project. He is driven to seek security by trying to reach self-sufficiency; but he is unable to reach genuine beatitude so long as he fails to center his life in God, whose nature is love.

Such contemporary theological commentators on the doctrine of man as Reinhold Niebuhr, Nicolas Berdyaev and Emil Brunner have freely abandoned certain aspects of these traditional teachings and retained others. Some of the notions which have been abandoned are: (1) there was a time in history when an individual named Adam enjoyed the sinless exercise of his human powers; (2) there was a later moment when he "fell"; (3) the resulting corruption has been seminally transmitted to his offspring; (4) all later individuals can be regarded as participating in Adam's guilt because he "contained" human nature within himself. Indeed, a literal interpretation of the story in Genesis runs into insuperable difficulties even if the natural sciences are ignored. For example, the more one ascribes perfection (original righteousness) to Adam, the more impossible does it become to conceive of how he *could* fall into sin. Prior to the disobedient act there had to be something wrong with him spiritually, something within him which was capable of succumbing to temptation. In that case the disobedient act fails to explain how he became (not just corruptible, but) actually "naughty" in his motives.

In view of its anachronistic associations, why bother to reformulate the doctrine at all? Why not, for the sake of clarity, abandon it entirely? Our answer is that imaginative vision in literature, philosophy and religion cannot be translated without loss into literal, rationalistic or scientific categories. Myths and symbols possess an evocative power which cannot be rivaled by the propositions of discursive thinking. Only by paying heed to them can one have access to the primordial feelings which have produced them and which they directly express; and some of these primordial feelings seem to be racial, not merely individual. An understanding of the symbolism which is associated with the doctrine of the *imago Dei* (and its analogues outside the Jewish-Christian tradition) is no more useless than an understanding of the Œdipus theme with Freud or the archetypes with Jung. Indeed, lack of such understanding can prevent one from taking due account of factors which profoundly influence human life even though they fall outside the confines of rationalistic thinking.

Moreover, which kind of language one regards as most adequate to express man's situation will depend upon preconceptions. From a naturalistic perspective, the language of vision in literature, philosophy and religion, tells us something interesting about the imaginary worlds which human wishes and needs have spun; but only scientific language is accurately geared to the structure of reality. From a theistic perspective, the language of drama and of personal relationships—struggle and triumph, anxiety and fellowship, guilt and forgiveness—will be regarded as fundamental. Scientific language will be regarded as an extremely valuable means of describing those aspects of reality, both internal and external to man, which can properly be treated as objects. But all facts and events which consist of objects will be regarded as abstractions from the fundamental situation of existing as a person in relation to other persons.

Actually, there is no escape from the language of vision if one attempts to deal at all with ultimate problems. Plato realized this when he introduced myths at points where he desired to write about the origin and destiny of the world-process or of the soul; and in our own century Spengler and Toynbee, among others, have discovered that the study of history cannot pass over into synoptic interpretation without the employment of similar devices. The extra-rational character of myths makes them treacherous, but it can also make them fruitful. Moreover, we should not overlook the extent to which seemingly literal, scientific philosophies are compelled to resort to them unawares. Take a phrase like "the emergence of man from nature." The instant that it is used as more than a descriptive truism, it employs "nature" as an explanatory concept prior to and apart from the advent of man, to account for how intricate physical, chemical and biological processes were conspiring to produce him. Scientific knowledge cannot provide us with this explanatory concept because it does not purport to discuss the ultimate origins of being. Nevertheless many naturalistic philosophers continually use "Nature" in the mythological sense while assuming that all their thinking remains within the confines of strictly scientific categories.

Within its own theological context, therefore, let us examine the implications of the Christian doctrine of the *imago Dei*. First, it provides a basis for the acceptance of creatureliness. It implies that there is nothing wrong with being finite, with having a body, with being this particular individual, with being subject to the vicissitudes of life and death in the environment of nature. Therefore the doctrine has been an important safeguard within the Christian tradition against all views which attempt to regard the finite, temporal world as unreal, the body as evil, and death as an incident which relieves man of a temporal encumbrance without touching the intrinsically immortal core of his soul.* From the point of view of modern thought generally, and from the point of view of psycho-analysis in particular, this implicit warning against trying to become "pure spirit" by escaping from time, particularity, and the fulfillment of natural conditions, should be acknowledged as an asset within the Christian view of man.

Some liberal Protestant interpretations construe the doctrine as meaning that man is "intrinsically divine." Hence they have supported the notion that the moral, spiritual part of man is his "real" nature, linking him to the invisible world, and that his bodily, animal nature must not be regarded as fundamental. The

---

*Greek theology, partly because of its affiliations with Platonic thought, lost sight of some of these points when it linked mortality to sin and held that, had it not been for sin, man would have been naturally immortal.

theory that man is "nice" at the core has, for obvious reasons, had tough sledding in recent years. Moreover, a mystical or idealistic employment of the notion of man's "divinity" easily slurs over the fact that the doctrine of the *imago Dei* is designed to stress the difference between the Creator and the creature as well as their similarity. Ironically enough, the liberal version is a vestige of Christian thought which has proven especially attractive to those humanists who are glad to affirm the divinity of man after having dispensed with the Deity.

The doctrine implies, in the second place, that man is a special sort of creature, significantly different from every other item, process or level in nature. Like other individual things, he has unity as a spatio-temporal phenomenon; but unlike them, he must *win* unity as a person. In him nature has turned reflexively upon itself and become self-conscious. He has the power to bind past, present and future together in a stable, organizing center of ongoing experience; the power to use the "shorthand" of conceptual thought, thus grasping universal principles in a single act of apprehension instead of having to move laboriously from one discrete particular to the next; the power to direct his action intentionally toward previsioned aims; the power to distinguish between beautiful and ugly, true and false, good and bad; the power to organize communities in accordance with meanings, so that individuals act in concert through symbols and ideas instead of being at the mercy of instinct; the power to be both actor and spectator in relation to his own existence. In these capacities, and the consequences which follow from them, nature reaches a special kind of fruition in man; for without him there would be only happenings instead of meanings. The universe becomes drenched with significance by passing into his consciousness. Man is "above" nature, even though he can never jump out of it.

Therefore, although there is nothing wrong with man's being a creature, he is the only "animal" for whom acceptance or rejection of his status can arise as a problem. The intelligence and freedom which are the marks of his grandeur are also the marks of his misery. The endowments of creativity carry with them the problem of what is to be done with them. The capacity to stand over against nature and one's own experience carries with it the possibility of estrangement and inner ambiguity.

Man is discontented with his status; yet unless he were capable of discontent he would not be human. He cannot maintain the unity he already has except by seeking for a unity which he does not yet fully possess. For example, unless he were aware of the split between subject and object, the driving motive behind science would never arise. The quest for truth is directed toward conformity between knowing and its objects, and through science a practical concordat can be effected between man's purposes and the dependable processes of nature. Yet the chasm between the activity of thinking and the objects it apprehends is frustrating as well as stimulating; there could be no quest for truth without the possibility of disastrous illusions and aching ignorance. Many philosophers, even hardheaded Aristotle, have perceived that there can be no perfect consummation of this quest except as the knower and the known become identical. Thinking points toward a goal which, if reached, would put an end to the necessity for thinking.

Consider one more example. Unless man were judge of his own actions, as well as doer, morality could not arise. Without sympathetic imagination and a vision of the good, he could make no headway toward reconciling conflicts within himself and in his society. Yet the interminable discrepancy between the ideal and the actual, which is the driving force behind all moral achievement, is a source of despair as well as inspiration. Morality also is pointed toward a goal which, if reached, would put an end to the necessity for moral striving.

Hence man cannot move a step toward self-knowledge except by employing endowments which he did not create, within the context of an origin he cannot fathom, directed toward a destiny he cannot descry. Nevertheless, he is a creature capable of creativeness, and his gifts are his to do with as he will. Persons, through decision, make history; nature, apart from persons, simply passes through change. Therefore, at the opposite extreme from trying to play God, man may come to regard himself as more impotent than he actually is. Ancient stories such as the Prometheus myth reflect the fact that man has viewed the autonomous exercise of his powers as dangerous.* Yet failure to find outlets for his creativity is just as perilous as the irresponsible employment of it.

In this connection many versions of the doctrine need to be corrected or expanded in the light of psychotherapy. Man's longing to exercise his creative powers should not be regarded necessarily as an indication of pride (*hybris*). And if his creativeness is to be "like God's," subject to ineradicable differences between Creator and creature, it can take forms which reflect man's affinity with the natural world which is God's handiwork. Both rigid moralism (operating all too often under the aegis of orthodox Christianity) and the doctrine of the transcendence of God have often been employed to repudiate elements of vitality and spontaneity in man which should be incorporated in the meaning of wholeness. A paralyzing conflict between arid virtue and wayward vitality should not be regarded as part and parcel of what it means to be limited and creaturely. On the contrary, it reflects failure on man's part to align himself aright with the divine vitality which moves through all growing, breathing things. The helplessness to which the doctrine of sin calls attention has far too often been conceived in such a way that the doctrine condemns, as an effort on man's part to "save himself," what is really indispensable to man's "being himself." Despite its acceptance of the goodness of creation, Christian theology has frequently allowed the doctrine of sin virtually to obliterate the first affirmation. The result is that one scolds himself, not merely for ego-centricity, but for being a self; he condemns not merely sexual excesses, but sexuality itself; he feels guilty, not merely for grasping at power unduly, but for asserting and maintaining his own existence at all. Repeatedly in the history of Christianity, the Church has sought to force artistic creativity, romantic love,

*Though Prometheus was not a summary symbol for Man, he was a Titan who put power in man's hands.

intellectual inquiry and the venturing spirit into preconceived molds; it has used these talents insofar as they could be subjugated to the Church's own conception of obedience to God, but it has steadily opposed them insofar as they refused to capitulate.

The regrettable alienation of modern culture from Christianity must be understood, in part, as a reaction against ecclesiastical shackles which, if they had not been thrown off, really would have prevented man from carrying through important forms of progress, enlightenment and self-understanding. The failure of Christianity to furnish an organic center for culture has meant that many of these potentially creative powers have run riot. Modern society, armed with technology and dreaming of self-sufficiency, has been set adrift to fashion its own gods and ideologies. These dreams have indeed brought our civilization to the edge of the abyss. But part of the explanation (how large a part, it is impossible to guess) lies in the fact that the Church, by labeling "sinful" human resources which are potentially creative, has failed to provide a religious framework within which these potentialities could be expressed and guided; as a consequence of their repudiation they have been driven into revolt and aggressiveness.*

Therefore theology should expand its conception of what is implied in man's creation in the image of God so as to make room for a thoroughgoing integration between natural vitality and rational order. It should expand its conception of those factors in human nature which can be used by God in overcoming sin; and, as we shall see, this may also involve some alterations in its conception of sin. Some of the derangement which goes into sin has been due, not to the fact that man has tried to save himself, but to the fact that his religion has taught him to regard as liabilities what are actually latent assets. A strategy which continues unqualifiedly to set the Church against the world will shut itself off from nurturing these resources for recovery and

---

*Because our concern is confined to the reinterpretation of a theological doctrine, I refrain from mentioning the secular causes of disintegration, some of which have already been indicated.

new life. If the Church is really interested in curing sin, instead of merely calling attention to its ineradicability, it will not despise the effective help which "worldly" agencies can offer, even though the agencies in question do not use the word "sin."

The image of integrity and innocence, wherein man lived in harmony with nature, his fellows and God, is nonsense if one tries to locate it literally in a primitive age at the dawn of history. But it is not nonsense if one takes it as indicative of every man's capacity and striving for such integrity and harmony. If it be true that man's finding of his place in the scheme of creation, so that he can be harmoniously related to nature, himself and his fellows, is contingent upon his being related harmoniously with God, then this fact is of paramount importance for the psychotherapist. For it implies that man's striving for psychic and spiritual health can be counted on, in the struggle against illness, insanity and evil, only because his essential nature is suited to an appropriate role in this scheme of creation, and because nature is suited to the emergence and sustenance of man. In a word, man need neither capitulate to nature nor defy it in order to be himself. The tragic struggle whereby he seeks to come to terms with life and destiny is not a lonely, transitory one, wherein for a brief period he creates *ex nihilo* whatever humane meaning existence can possess; for this struggle is an integral part of a cosmic creativity. The buried resources are "there," so that they can be drawn upon, only because of a divine strategy which reaches back beyond the appearance of man upon this planet. Man is in his own body and mind a compendium of every preceding "level" of evolution—physical, chemical, biological and psychological. The resources he draws upon, in seeking to become at one with himself, are not merely "his"; they are rooted in the whole creation, which is grounded in God. Therefore man can become at one with himself only by finding his place in a harmony much wider than himself; but this harmony is not "pre-established"; he has a share in winning, in actualizing, it. He cannot fulfill his own nature unless his capacities gain free expression; but neither can he fulfill his own nature unless his freedom is brought into right relationship with God.

CHAPTER VI

Moralism

THE CONCEPT OF responsibility has been a source of endless difficulties in psychology, philosophy and theology. Any one who has pondered the problem of freedom and determinism will probably sympathize with the sentiment which prompted Milton to assign discussion of this topic to some little devils in Satan's legions who liked to bandy it about during moments of relaxation —without getting anywhere. Nevertheless, psychotherapy has thrown light upon the problem by uncovering the manner in which we are determined by unconscious forces. Its findings point to a form of self-determinism. The self is not merely the passive resultant of inherited constitution plus environmental influences; it builds up an internal unity of its own which enters actively as well as passively into interplay with the surrounding world and other persons. Yet the character-structure being what it is at a given moment, the thoughts, feelings and actions of that moment follow necessarily. This does not imply that the character-structure cannot change, radically and fundamentally; but it does imply that such changes are "law-abiding" in the sense that they come about in response to specific conditions. Psychotherapy interprets particular responses, however, in the light of the whole self's striving to reach or maintain a workable balance between this internal structure and external events. As enriched by the discoveries of psycho-somatic medicine, it sees each "level" within man's psycho-physical organism as affected by every other level. Therefore, it does not fall into the reductionist mistake of talking as though physiological processes or psychological mechanisms were isolable items, each possessing a specific gravity of its own, which, when arranged in a certain way, automatically pro-

94

duce thoughts and actions. Psychotherapy is one version of modern psychology which cannot get along without the "psyche." It sees physical, biological and unconscious processes as participating in the life of a self which is held together, in the end, by consciousness and purposiveness. Indeed, unless the therapist believed that conscious intention can influence events he could not carry on his work at all.

Because psychotherapy is committed to the increase of man's capacity to achieve responsibility, it must oppose those forms of psychology which, when taken seriously, spread the illusion that man is an automaton. Yet because it is determinist, it assumes that what is called "moral wrong," as well as mental and physical disease, must be regarded as the necessary consequence, in a given moment, of the interplay between a formed character-structure and an external situation. This does not mean that the distinction between what man can help and what he cannot help disappears entirely; but it does mean that some of our ideas concerning *how* man can alter conditions may have to be revised.

Christian theology has produced many theories, of course, concerning freedom and determinism; but we shall confine our attention to two major trends, discussing the first in this chapter and the second in the next. The first holds that each child comes into the world free from hereditary guilt, and that every man possesses free will in such a fashion that, whenever matters of right and wrong are at stake, he can make his own choice. The most famous advocate of this theory, Pelagius, was an earnest, practically minded moralist who was convinced that men could promote good ends if they tried hard enough; therefore, he sought to close off the "excuse" that they are compelled to do evil by sinful predispositions. He regarded the road to good character as marked by a steady effort of will whereby an individual makes the rational and ethical parts of himself dominant over his lower nature.

The second theory might be called "theological determinism," or "bondage to original sin." Variant forms of it can be found in St. Paul, Augustine, Luther and Calvin. Basically it holds that because human nature has been corrupted at the center, no effort of will can suffice to bring about a radical change of heart. Therefore, no man can save himself, no man can make himself righteous. He can be released from bondage to sin only by a power stronger than himself (God); and the transformation which comes about through being forgiven and redeemed by God is a gift, it cannot be earned. Christ, by taking human nature upon Himself and by conquering sin's power, has made available to all men who trust in Him a spiritual and ethical emancipation which they could not possibly achieve by themselves. In fairness to Pelagians we should add that they do not deny the need for divine grace through Christ; but they have regarded this assistance primarily as taking the form of an inspiring moral example. According to the second type of theology, however, the old, corrupt self, which was in bondage to sin, must be replaced by a "new creation"—that rectified human nature which has been instituted by Christ in perfect union with God. This new human nature remains, therefore, a gift, sustained by the indwelling Spirit of Christ working in the hearts of believers through the Christian community; it is not man's property.

One more distinction needs to be made. In the Pelagian view the individual is conceived atomistically; neither hereditary factors nor what we would now call "social conditioning" can rob him of free will. A person may be helped by following worthy examples or harmed by imitating unworthy ones; but nothing forces him to turn toward one or the other; the choice, in any instance, is at his own disposal. The second theory, on the other hand, is much more capable of taking into account the fateful way in which every child is influenced by both heredity and society before he has an opportunity to exercise moral discrimination.

We are now ready to appraise Pelagian moralism in the light of psychotherapy. It rests on the familiar conception of "will power" as something whereby the individual can force himself in any direction he wants to go. This conception underlies moralism generally, whether associated with religious beliefs or not.

It assumes that man can live up to any ideal or law that is obligatory upon him. He fulfills what he ought to do by making the principles of reason and conscience triumph over the irrational and sensuous elements in his make-up. Psychotherapeutic findings indicate, however, that this sort of an organization of the self is not "free" at all. On the contrary, it represents a continual condition of internal division and strife. The moralistic individual has not made fully "his own" the ideals which he strives to promote, and they fail to satisfy important needs and capacities. The more he has to force himself by conscientious effort, the more something in him is obviously resisting. The attempt to become virtuous *against* one's "wants" instead of by transformation of them is foredoomed to failure, and the history of moralism illustrates the failure. Ethical standards are insecure so long as they can be enforced only through coercion and conflict-ridden conscientiousness. Resistance to them gathers momentum, underneath the surface; and the more pressure is exerted to hold these resistances in check, the more explosive and disruptive is their rebellion whenever they find an opportunity to break loose. In at least two ways, the ideals toward which a moralistic individual directs his will power are compulsive instead of free. First, they represent the internalization of authoritarian standards instead of his own responsible judgment. If they represented the latter, the forcing would not be necessary. Second, the strenuousness with which he imposes them upon himself reflects the amount of energy that must be expended in overcoming resistance. The "moral energy" which the individual may interpret as manifesting singleness of purpose is precisely correlated with the strength of the psychic forces ranged against his conscience. And moral effort can do nothing to reduce the pressure from the latter because the individual's consciousness is out of touch with them and wants to avoid recognizing their existence and power.

Once moralism gets established, a person feels quite sincerely that it is worth the price—especially in view of the fact that apparently he has no other alternative unless he wants to "go to pot." In return for holding himself in line, he receives a good opinion of himself, and a good reputation in the community. Almost everything he prizes, including his own sense of direction, would be jeopardized if he became seriously skeptical about the soundness of the methods and standards he uses. All of the advantages of moralism are immediately obvious, tangible and important; most of the price he is paying is hidden. The price may include a sacrifice in whole-heartedness, deep friendship, full experience of both the bodily and the spiritual riches of human love, steady joy in living, the unforced employment of talents he already possesses, and the development of interests which have never been given a chance. The price may also include psychosomatic ills which he does not remotely associate with his moralism.

The fact that there may be many inclinations which go counter to his virtuous actions (such as hostility accompanying the "generous" deed) can easily be discounted. Even if he is aware of them (and he usually is not), he can say to himself: "Well, I did the right thing, didn't I? I put the base motives aside, didn't I?" By such methods he can succeed indefinitely in avoiding the full truth about the condition of his "heart," because externally his actions remain so consistently correct. One of the disturbing things about Jesus was that he punctured moralism by looking behind the deed to the spirit in which it is done.

An important qualification must be added, however. Undeniably there are times in any one's life when carrying out a given line of duty, which one espouses as a whole, involves specific segments that are extremely distasteful. One can promote the end-result only by performing tasks some of which are repugnant. Under such circumstances, one has to use "will power" to go ahead; but the ultimate aim is accepted freely, not compulsively.

In contrast with moralism's generalizations about free will, psychotherapy leads to the conclusion that human beings use whatever freedom they possess, but that they differ tremendously in the degree to which they have reached that internal harmony on which freedom is based. Only in extremely pathological cases, of course, is behavior wholly compulsive. The extent to which a man can take responsibility for his attitudes and actions varies directly with the extent to which he is aware of his total motivation. The more conscience and impulse are in conflict with each other, the more compulsive does the expression of both become. Therefore, the road to freedom is to be followed not by "putting on the pressure," but by an expansion of self-acquaintance—including aspects of oneself which are ordinarily regarded as unworthy and dangerous. As we have seen, the latter method may uncover such startling and irrational tendencies that initially it seems merely to increase one's bondage to evil, while having reduced the old moralistic "drive" which kept such evil in check. In some cases this terrifying transitional stage is unavoidable because the organization of motivation is thrown back to an earlier stage of life. Figuratively speaking, the individual is taking off a strait jacket which has been holding him upright all his life, and he is like an infant who is learning to walk on his own ethical legs for the first time. The situation may not be as bad as that, however. The removal of the strait jacket and the development of independent strength can take place *pari passu,* with the latter taking over gradually as the former disappears. Yet it must be recognized that, through no fault of theirs, psychoanalysts find it impossible to help people become aware of their previous bondage without running the risk of releasing rebellious forces. In the first seizures of rebellion the patient may burst into forms of immorality which do not represent the style of life he will adopt when he has attained integrity. Episodes of this sort should not blind us to the fact that analysis is aimed at a transformation of conscience, not an eradication of it.*

Psychotherapy also stands in contrast to moralism insofar as the latter rests on an atomistic view of the self. Every therapist knows that the moral capacities and incapacities of the individ-

*In the textbooks, a man who is devoid of conscience is called a "psychopathic personality," and it is one of the most difficult disorders to deal with. The individual is in a state of infantile obliviousness to all inhibitions, social standards and responsibility.

ual are so powerfully determined by his constitution and formed character-structure that often the only way to alter the effects of early conditioning involves his retracing the past, in feeling as well as in thought. Even then, of course, he does not cease to be the person who was thus conditioned by his past; but many influences and experiences, including the most injurious (traumatic), can be modified when they are taken into the context of adult life, instead of remaining buried back in childhood when he was incapable of understanding them and helpless in the face of them.

An illustration derived from case material will serve to clarify the point. (1) The patient begins the analysis declaring that he has been brought up in a fine home and has a deep affection for his parents. (2) In the process of getting light on his own problems he discovers the extent to which his parents' neuroses have contributed to the development of his own. (3) He recalls specific instances of parental domination in connection with incidents where he felt guilty for disobeying them; but he now realizes that their demands were arbitrary and stupid. (4) He has an uncontrollable upsurge of hatred for one or both of his parents; he blames them for everything. (5) He gradually discovers that, although they may be responsible for what was done to him before he could defend himself, he is now responsible for whatever continuing effect these attitudes have in the present. (6) As he realizes how difficult it is for him to "do anything about it," he begins to realize that his parents were "caught," just like most people. (7) Growing comprehension of his own difficulties results in growing tolerance toward his parents in the midst of their difficulties. (8) Once he has achieved independence, he realizes that they can no longer dominate him, and the way is open for the establishment of a new relationship of mutual respect and affection between him and his parents on the basis of adult equality instead of on the basis of compliance-defiance.

This illustration has been deliberately oversimplified, and it sounds, perhaps, too pretty. Yet two aspects of the process it describes are worth special attention. In the first place, at no point does the individual cease to be conditioned by his own past; nevertheless, he can significantly change his relationship to that past. In the second place, the ideal of family affection with which he started was not wholly abandoned. His affection for his parents was made less ambiguous by *facing* the hatreds and feelings of guilt with which it was originally entangled, instead of holding them out of awareness for the sake of being a loyal child. The genuineness of his affection was actually increased when he ceased trying to make himself and his parents out to be more worthy than they were. It became adult and humane through recognizing shortcomings all around, instead of through ignoring them.

Without departing from determinism, therapy makes possible emancipation from bondage to social conditioning as mediated, in our illustration, through the family. By generalizing on this basis we can understand how collective evils get transmitted from one generation to the next. In fact, many of us need to make a transition in relation to the ideologies and moralistic assumptions of our culture which is analogous to the transition just described in relation to family influences. A great deal of what passes for soundness in economic, political and ethical thinking is just as compulsive and bogus as our patient's initial "love" for his parents. A mature attitude toward social axioms and pressures can be established only when the individual has reached a position where he can conform or resist responsibly; where he knows, that is, why he is doing either one; and where he is able to anticipate the consequences accurately, and is willing to accept them. Note that such a conception of responsibility is as much opposed to compulsive rebellion against society as it is to compulsive conformism.

An atomistic theory of "free will" cannot attach sufficient gravity to the communal aspect of moral evil and mental illness. Much moralistic exhortation is entirely futile because it urges the individual to make a stand against given social evils, without taking into account the fact that his relationship to the community has enmeshed him emotionally in those evils in a fashion which is quite beyond the reach of his voluntary control. Perhaps large segments of our population are so "uneducated" or "insensitive" that it would be folly to expect them to set forth on their own high road of ethical heroism in any case. But it is also true of many of the "educated" and "sensitive" that they go through the motions of following a strict code whenever their interests are at stake, but find great relief in taking a holiday from the code whenever they can get away from their home towns. Whether among the "uneducated" or the "educated," the widespread moral infantilism of our society must be attributed in part to the fact that we are trained from childhood to believe that ethical standards are something the anonymous "they" expect of us instead of something we can make our own. The pathway to a vigorous, self-maintaining and developing morality involves, not imposition from the top, but enhancement of personal responsibility through every level of the population. The most acute problems facing civilization are connected with the fact that many economic, political and religious forces are driving mankind toward regimentation, for the sake of "security"(?). A radical break with these collectivist patterns can come about only through a rapid and widespread growth of democratic beliefs and feelings "in the guts."

Psychotherapeutic findings can be used helpfully as one tries to confront the predicament of man in a communal, instead of a purely individual, context. The path of human development starts, inevitably, in a condition of undifferentiated dependence upon the group (the primitive "We"). Unless the process of development is blocked, the normal individual goes through a gradual consolidation of independence and self-consciousness, becoming a unique center of organized thought, feeling and initiative. Yet he reaches maturity, not by maintaining his isolation, but by being able to establish relations of mutual support and co-operation with the community (the adult "We"), without relinquishment of individual responsibility. The anxieties of our age have driven many men regressively away from individual freedom into primitive forms of group solidarity. But we cannot fully understand this "escape from freedom" unless we recognize the extent to which our rationalistic, externalized, individualistic culture has failed to provide man with the kind of communal solidarity and collective loyalty which might lead his freedom forward instead of backward. Nationalism, with its obvious perils, and a highly commendable but embryonic form of internationalism, are the principal secular objects toward which men can direct their communal fidelities today. Generalized loyalties to science, art, or progress are attenuated as compared with the emotional power generated by divisive forms of communal loyalty. Hence even the best secular ideals do not fully satisfy man's need for relating individual life organically to the life of the race. The kind of solidarity worthy of complete devotion cannot be actualized by a single nation, a single civilization, or a single epoch of history. If ultimate loyalty is to be directed toward an ideal incarnate in a community, instead of toward ideals which remain abstract, that community must be potentially universal. This is a religious need, and criticism of existing Churches is barren unless it acknowledges that a religious community which enhances, instead of stultifying, individual responsibility is the only adequate remedy for the spiritual isolation of modern man.

CHAPTER VII

Bondage to Sin

AT CERTAIN POINTS there is a remarkable parallel between the Pauline-Augustinian conception of original sin and the psycho-analytic conception of neurosis. Freud more than once called attention to the parallel. In both instances man finds himself in a condition of inner conflict, and filled with hatred, envy and mistrust toward his neighbors. In both instances it is the basic condition that is enslaving; particular "sins" or "symptoms" are peripheral effects deriving from this central cause, and particular "good deeds" make little dent upon the basic condition. In both instances the injurious influences of others are seen to be so interwoven with personal reactions that it is almost impossible to differentiate between them. Similarly, it is almost impossible to disentangle the respects in which a man has fallen into sin (or neurosis) by necessity or through his own "fault." In both instances the central problem cannot be solved merely by an effort of will; insofar as it ever gets solved at all, the solution comes about through a change in the "will" itself.

Despite the fact that it is deterministic, going hand in hand with belief in predestination, the Christian doctrine of original sin does not abrogate the conception of personal responsibility. On the contrary, it holds that men are "without excuse" because they possess the capacity to distinguish between good and evil. They sin knowingly. Psychotherapeutic concepts express matters differently; yet insofar as an attempt is made through them to retain some notion of responsibility, instead of falling into sheer fatalism, the same theoretical dilemma arises. How combine responsibility with determinism?

Among the various explanations of moral evil, there are three especially which call for attention. Advocates of the Christian doctrine of original sin ordinarily hold that, although all three of these explanations throw some light on the problem, they must not be permitted to "explain away" the individual's proclivity to evil. First, the social theory of moral evil. From Rousseau to Marx, and before and after both, there have been thinkers who regarded the individual as an innocent victim of enslaving social maladjustments. Second, the "evolutionary lag" theory. Here man is seen as having gradually to make rational principles dominant over animal impulses. It is not his fault that this is a slow business; it is not his fault that he carries with him a bodily and emotional equipment which betray how recently (geologically speaking) he emerged from the primeval forest; it is not his fault that he must struggle upward toward a humane ethic against the drag of impulses that reflect Darwinian principles. Third, what might be called the "Socratic-Deweyan" theory. Moral evil is due to ignorance. Insofar as man understands the good, he will do it. Hence moral evil will largely disappear as soon as we have reached adequate scientific understanding and control in connection with psychological and sociological phenomena.

From the theological standpoint which we shall examine in this chapter, none of these explanations, nor all of them put together, face fully the seriousness of man's predicament. Nor do they succeed in locating the central source of the trouble. The first fails to explain why there is something in the individual which succumbs to and strings along with the evils that are labeled "social maladjustment." It fails to explain how individuals "got that way" in the first place, and it fails to give an adequate account of why they tend to stay "that way." In short, how can social evils become established and maintain themselves unless there is something in individuals, from one generation to the next, which provides fertile soil for the seeds of evil?

The second explanation regards man's intelligence and imagination as good, and attributes his misdeeds to his body and his animal impulses. Thus it rests upon a highly questionable dualism which may lead to a repudiation of the body, and to the construction of an idealistic ethic that fails to take account of man's need for psycho-physical wholeness. Even when these mistakes do not occur, the theory is defective because it leaves out of account those forms of evil which cannot be attributed to the corrupting or impeding influences of the body. Such evils spring from a perverted employment of the supposedly "good" parts of man—his intelligence and imagination. In short, if the man is evil, his condition will manifest itself in abuses of his "spiritual" as well as of his "physical" capacities.

The third explanation is defective because it fails to cover the evils that are due to a bad will instead of to ignorance. The expansion of science cannot by itself remove those evils which are due, not to inadequate study of empirical data or false thinking, but to bad motivation. We cannot be unqualifiedly happy about the progress of science unless we know what it will be used for; and that depends upon the moral character and insight of the men who possess such knowledge, not merely upon their expertness as scientists. Science, in itself, is morally neutral; the same knowledge and skill can be used to murder or heal, to regiment or emancipate, to bomb or to bless. It can be used in an indispensable way to implement whatever moral aims we espouse; but it cannot, by itself, determine what those aims should be.

The missing factor, in all three of these explanations, is "bondage of the will"; and the attempt to throw the whole blame on factors outside of the individual or outside the "good" part of himself, is an escape mechanism. Yet it is at this point that the paradox of determinism-and-responsibility arises for theological thinking. If man is caught, not merely by external circumstances beyond his control, but by internal bondage to a predisposition to evil, then how can he take responsibility for the latter? The Christian doctrine asserts that man becomes caught in bondage to his own nature, not because the nature he has received from God is evil, but because man makes it evil himself. As we have seen, the most influential contemporary statements of the doctrine do not contemplate a chronology wherein man started, historically, as good, and then became evil through his own act. They conceive of every human being as finding himself in a setting, from birth to death, wherein he is continually violating his own good nature, not merely because he is ignorant of what he ought to do, or because social and physical influences prevent him from doing what he ought, but because he *will* not do it. Yet he is so enslaved to this evil will that he cannot unfetter himself by an act of will; for every act of will issues from a center that is already wrongly disposed. If one asks how, temporally speaking, he got into the position where his will was thus rebelliously fixed, most writers on the problem agree that there is no answer.* They agree that every particular refusal to follow the good presupposes a will which is already set in such refusal. As Kierkegaard put it: "Sin presupposes itself." Yet these same writers insist that continuation in bondage to sin is carried forward responsibly, not ignorantly or automatically.

This ingrained and inescapable self-centeredness constitutes alienation from God. God's love, being perfect, is free from the distortions that result from seeking one's own advantage over others and from attaching undue importance to one's own concerns (*e.g.*, possessions, ambitions, family, nation, etc.—just because they belong to "me"). God's love is forthgoing and sacrificial—and all human egocentricity is at war with it.

Our discussion of salvation must be reserved for another chapter; but it should be noted at this point that it is not the intention of the theologian or of the gospel he expounds to leave man in this hopeless predicament. Indeed, the theologian has not invented the doctrine at all. It has grown up because it has described accurately the situation in which spiritually sensitive men have found themselves; and the more insight they possessed, the more inescapable have such descriptions of their plight become. They "know" the good, in the sense that they are adequately

*Incidentally Kant, who for the most part followed a moralistic view in his ethical and theological thinking, is more in line with recent interpretations of the doctrine of original sin at this point. In his *Religion within the Limits of Reason Alone* he holds that the origins of moral evil must lie beyond temporal categories.

aware of what their motives and actions should be; and yet something stronger than their own wills prevents them from having such motives and from carrying out such actions. Nevertheless, this somber diagnosis is not an end-in-itself. Its chief value lies in the fact that only one who has been awakened to the full seriousness of his own guilt, and his own inability to overcome it, is in a position to look for and to accept the only adequate remedy—namely, the saving power of God's love and forgiveness in Jesus Christ, whereby He does something for us which we cannot do for ourselves. God alone could create us in the first place, and He alone can "recreate" (regenerate) us. Thus an awareness of the radical character of the problem goes hand in hand with an awareness of the radical character of the remedy. So long as one assumes that odd bits of tinkering with one's character-structure may do the job, or that with a little more effort, a little more enlightenment, and a firm faith in man's goodness, everything will somehow turn out all right, awareness of the need for faith in God's redemptive power will not arise. Hence rejection of the uncomfortable notion that man is caught in a dilemma which he cannot solve by means of his own energy and ingenuity is explicable in terms of his intense need to hang onto the illusion of self-sufficiency. The refusal to admit how deeply in the wrong he is, and how much he needs help, is symptomatic of the basic problem. If he were able to repent, and to admit (as Alcoholics Anonymous do) that only some divine power "greater than himself" can save him, he would already be in a condition of humility, moral realism and readiness for faith.

The motive behind the doctrine of sin, then, is not to drive in a sense of despair and insufficiency just because one enjoys seeing men wriggle in agony. The motive behind it is to reach full awareness of the depth of the human problem. It is folly to say that we should not feel guilty when we look back on our own lives, leaving nothing out. The sense of guilt is a sign that we have not become totally insensitive, hardened and irrecoverable. And what else can one feel or should one feel as he thinks of the collective crimes of war and injustice in which he is directly or indirectly implicated? Despair may indeed accompany this awareness of guilt, and, if a way is not found to some saving resolution of the problem, such despair can be ruinous. In other words the path from bondage to salvation is painful, and bordered with spiritual perils. An intensified sense of sin, without the saving release which comes from realizing that one does *not* have to overcome the sin by himself before he can find forgiveness and reconciliation with God, is the curse of legalism. But when despair and contrition lead to full trust in God, the individual is rescued from self-condemnation and from the hopeless task of trying to cure his own bad conscience by making himself righteous.

In the foregoing paragraphs, I have attempted to state the theological case in its strongest form, omitting some elements which patently express self-hatred and contempt for mankind, and also omitting some of the doctrinal devices which have been used to frighten and threaten men into the acceptance of what is supposedly a serene and joyful faith. The question might still arise as to whether these omitted features have not built up such ineradicable connotations around the word "sin" that it would be better to abandon the term entirely if one wants to avoid having imputed to him the cruelty and morbidity which have been associated with it. But that is a verbal question which can be left aside as we turn to a psychological critique of the essential issues.

From a psychological standpoint there can be little quarrel with an attempt to take full account of the seriousness and stubbornness of those factors in the individual and in society which lead to misery, hopelessness, anxiety, self-aggrandizement, inferiority feelings, the tyrannical conscience on the one hand and stuffy complacency on the other, crime, insanity, race-prejudice, economic injustice and war—no matter what terms one uses. Psychotherapy itself does not draw a pretty picture of what lies in the unconscious; nor does it adopt a rosy view of man's status and prospects in his struggle to reach some measure of security and integrity. Caught as he is between imperious libidinal drives and the restricting stabilities of civilization, each man must grope toward a precarious balance between some measure of aggressive self-expression, without which he cannot live at all, and some measure of inhibition, without which he cannot live as a socialized human being. He has to steer a middle course between the anarchic riot of the *id* and the potentially stifling restrictions of the *super-ego*. And the battle between these conflicting sides of his nature may literally tear him apart, if he fails to reach a manageable equilibrium. Often he reaches such equilibrium only *by means of* neurosis. And many circumstances of contemporary life, such as concentration camps and military combat, impose stresses under which even the strongest *egos* finally break down.

Thus psychotherapy can, from one standpoint, be regarded as documenting to the full, and widening our awareness of, what the human race is up against in attempting to reach inner freedom and social security. It offers clinical details on some matters of which the fathers of the Church were either completely ignorant or only vaguely aware in their description of human ills and perversities. Yet, strikingly enough, the means which have been employed in exploring the seriousness of the situation have at the same time been instruments of healing. If psychotherapy has widened our acquaintance with the ramifications of "sin," it has at the same time widened our conceptions of how this bondage can be overcome. It is as though a full awareness of what is involved in being in psychological fetters were a key that opens the lock.

Strictly speaking, sin is alienation from God and is therefore not a merely psychological category. Nevertheless, psychology can be used to advantage in attempting to reach a sound doctrine of sin, relieved of harmful encumbrances. Such a doctrine would include at least the following observations: (1) Evasion of responsibility aggravates a problem or delays its solution. (2) A full awareness of personal limitations, and contrition for those which are alterable, are preconditions of moral improvement. (3) The social ramifications of evil, which run far beyond what the individual can control or alter, violate our conceptions of what life could and should be like; therefore, even at those points where one has to "accept" them, the acceptance is not simple acceptance. (4) When sin is faced in a personal relationship of trust, a man may be enabled to "do something" (by a method which is the reverse of moralistic effort) about problems he was previously impotent to solve.

It follows from these observations, however, that many of the attempts to convict men of sin which the Church has used are harmful. The facing of shortcomings—especially those which the individual cannot overcome—is never constructive except as he is allowed to uncover his problems in his own way. When some one else attempts to tell him what his deficiencies are, it makes no difference whether the individual agrees with the other's judgment or disagrees; he is deprived of that opportunity for first-hand insight which is an indispensable part of the healing process. Furthermore, this facing of shortcomings is never constructive unless it can be carried through in a situation where a man is accepted in spite of them, and where the remedy, insofar as one is forthcoming, consists of a dynamic realignment within the person himself instead of something imposed upon him from outside. Many people are repelled by the theological doctrine just outlined because it looks to them like an effort to force men into a specious situation of hopeless guilt for the sake of forcing them to accept a specious means of rescue.

Besides these practical criticisms, there are theoretical objections to be considered. It is hard to blame any psychologist for feeling that the Christian interpretation of man we have been following takes away with one hand what it holds out with the other. The doctrine of the *imago Dei* asserts that man's distinctive capacities are intrinsically good, and that awareness of moral distinctions rests upon them. But the doctrine of original sin asserts that the instant man employs these capacities he does so sinfully. How is one to disentangle what is intrinsically good from its spoliation? Man is a finite creature who must struggle to maintain his own existence; therefore a measure of "self-interest" is healthy and blameless. The will to live, creative expression of individuality, special devotion to family, friends, vocation and nation—all these are appropriate to man's situation, and linked to his God-given endowments. To say that pursuit of them must inevitably spring from a sinful center seems tantamount to a repudiation of human nature as such. It seems like condemning man, not merely for being illegitimately selfish and aggressive, but for being human at all.

Furthermore, if the individual is so trapped that he *cannot* will the good, then it matters little whether the enslaving factors are located primarily inside or outside himself; it is unfair, and entirely fruitless, to blame him for his failure. The doctrine of sin may rightly call attention to the fact that often men are not as free as they think they are. It may rightly hold that inner conflict, which is a major source of moral blindness and ineffectuality, cannot be overcome merely by an effort of will. But there is nothing to be said for it, and everything to be said against it, insofar as it instills or increases feelings of guilt for something we cannot help.

We must now attempt the difficult task of adjudicating between the foregoing theological and psychological arguments, without glozing over points where the disagreement may turn out to be ineradicable. In any interpretation of man there are, obviously, two possibilities of error. The first is to underestimate or fail to implement those resources of health and recovery which are actually available and the enhancement of which is desperately needed. To regard any situation prematurely as insoluble, because of a doctrinaire assumption about the intrinsic wickedness of human nature, is enervating and potentially disastrous. The main purpose in refusing to fool ourselves concerning the gravity of what we are up against is to channel our energies and quicken our resolution in whatever directions may go farthest toward coping with the situation. Psychotherapy has made an important contribution toward increasing man's capacity to solve his own problems, both by deepening the diagnosis and by tapping hitherto latent resources. And from this standpoint, theology richly deserves criticism wherever it has equated human "goodness" with slavish dependence upon the arbitrary will of a celestial tyrant who treats His creatures in a way that any humane person would regard as abominable. It deserves criticism wherever it represents God as wanting a kind of submission which would exclude man from participating in the discovery and actualization of his own beatitude.

The second possibility of error, however, (especially from the theologian's standpoint) is one of exaggerating the extent to which man can solve the problem of evil "on his own." In this connection, psychotherapy seems to align itself with one or more of the three explanations of evil which have already been criticized. At least, so long as the therapist's philosophical outlook is naturalistic, he is likely to feel that, everything considered, man has done quite creditably. For centuries cultural patterns have just "growed," like Topsy. Amidst the laws which govern the maintenance or the destruction of a clan, a nation, an empire, each generation has had to socialize its infants in such a way that there would be protection for the group against enemies from without and disruptive forces from within. The resulting tensions between the will to live and the will to co-operate, between hostility and love, between isolation and fellowship have been inevitable. An effective understanding of how to handle these tensions less destructively has been reached so recently, and is still so scantily dispersed, that no better result has been possible. So far as the contemporary situation is concerned, it is no one's fault that the *timing* has put technological power into man's hands faster than he has been able to carry forward a social evolution which would enable him to employ it without encountering the terrible risks which now confront him. The therapist is convinced that if what he and the social scientists now know, or are learning, can be given adequate implementation, then modern history will confirm the fact that man is "good" when given a decent chance. Even if he believes that the likelihood of a happy outcome is remote, the therapist may add that attempts to invoke divine aid merely run away from the problem and do nothing to reduce its gravity.

Yet from a theological standpoint it is impossible to overlook the symptoms of "hoping-against-hope" which accompany such an attitude. Knowledge of untapped resources in man leads to the hope that they can be implemented fast enough to avert disaster because, from a naturalistic or humanistic perspective, there is nothing else to place one's hopes in. It is also impossible to overlook the way in which supposedly impartial, scientific judgments concerning man's limitations, capacities and prospects fit with suspicious neatness into a general ideology which is simply "modern," and not peculiar to psycho-analysis at all. With a few exceptions, the psycho-analytic movement has concentrated upon the emancipation of man from prescientific moralistic and religious fetters. It has not looked at the other side of the picture, namely, the extent to which the worst diseases of modernity have been connected with a worship of human self-sufficiency. In one sense, to be sure, the therapist understands these diseases better than any one else, and he wants to divert human energy from idolatrous fixation upon the interests of a particular race, nation or class so that they can be directed to inclusive, humane ends. But his outlook is defective at that point where he is held captive in the mentality which worships "the best in man"—as though one could stop there. Without quarreling with the ethical content of his vision of the good for man, one must nevertheless point out that this content is left hanging in a cosmic vacuum. And one must add that there is little prospect of making inclusive, humane aims more potent than the immediate, compelling pressures of nationalism, totalitarianism and the class struggle unless they can capture the religious energies of men. In the end, these religious energies can be turned from unworthy objects to a worthy one only by refusing to deify human qualities and purposes, and by directing them, instead, to God Himself, in whom human freedom and beatitude are grounded.

Here we see how impossible it is to dodge theological issues in the course of attempting to specify what "human beatitude" means, what constitutes "full" awareness of man's predicament, and what "the available resources" are. The strongest theological argument, in my judgment, takes the form of holding that Christian belief provides a basis for the affirmation of human possibilities *as grounded in God* which humanism lacks. Confidence that man can move toward harmony between biological and moral factors makes sense, in the end, only if the dynamic structures which undergird such harmony are more far-reaching than anything man alone can determine or control. Nature, as science conceives of it, does not provide an adequate basis for belief in this coincidence. As man contributes to this coincidence he fulfills "his own" nature, but this fulfillment involves the unfoldment of possibilities which man alone cannot invent or create. In short, a naturalistic or humanistic outlook cannot do justice to the fact that man tends toward his own beatitude only as human good is made integral with its cosmic ground. Unless man discovers and accepts this integration, it cannot be actualized positively. Hence we have a right to reject any theology which ignores or belittles man's participation; we can even say that man "creates" value, in the sense that without him it cannot be actualized. But he does not create the resources on which he draws in playing this role.

Even when working within a humanistic perspective, a therapist cannot avoid trying to formulate a conception of human beatitude which rises above individual and cultural conditioning, though neither can he ignore or discount the importance of such conditioning. He does not regard man as he now is, or has been in the past, as indiscriminately trustworthy. The "human nature" which he is concerned to see expressed more fully can be defined only in terms of an *ideal* which he believes can be realized, or worked toward effectively. This ideal, based upon those elements of health which are to some extent at work in most men and are supremely embodied in a few, presupposes a transformation—a conversion. His attempt, as a scientist, to keep this norm closely related to expanding empirical information is altogether sound; and this is a feature of modern psychology from which theologians have much to learn. Because such a norm is flexible, it can remain relevant to changing circumstances and growing knowledge. Nevertheless it involves a synoptic vision of "the good for man" on the basis of which one discriminates between what is constructive and what is destructive among the forces that are studied empirically. If the norm is to be universally valid, instead of being merely a projection of the therapist's personal preferences, it must faithfully reflect the status of human values in relation to cosmic process as a whole. At this point the therapist can hardly avoid placing some sort of confidence in what has produced man, as well as in man himself. Extra-human factors have a direct bearing upon man's success and failure as he engages in the task of transforming himself. Such self-sufficiency as man can attain is reached within the context of this ultimate dependence.

If this context of ultimate dependence is conceived of in terms of cosmic indifference, then man's task of self-transformation and fulfillment must be carried on *against* and *despite* it. It is difficult to see how such a philosophy can at the same time stress the continuity between nature and man, though it usually does. Nevertheless let us grant that, despite certain puzzling features, such a philosophy does not make life wholly meaningless. If it is right, it has the virtue of not representing man's position as more secure than it actually is. It invites us to take up the risky, tragic "everyman's burden" of *bestowing* on life the only securities and meanings it can possess. These are fragile and fleeting; but they can be noble and satisfying while they last. We cannot change the odds against us. We have no alternative—except ignobility, whimpering and illusion.

Religious apologists have frequently made the mistake of deprecating what can be built upon such a foundation; they have been unduly anxious to expose the pride in humanistic thinking and to ignore the courage and honesty it may embody. But if the humanistic orientation is wrong, then notice the consequences. It shuts man off from a wider and more ultimate form of security which need not fall into wishful thinking or slavish dependence; religious security is his legitimate birthright so long as belief in God undergirds the growth of human responsibility, instead of being used to invoke a magic Helper. And even though humanism may open the way to honesty and fellowship at the human level, it shuts man off from communion with the divine source of personal integrity and of interpersonal love. Finally, it gives man nothing but himself and a vision of human possibilities to worship. Without detracting from the gratitude we may feel toward others, and even toward ourselves, we find at this point, supremely, that the religious inadequacy of humanism becomes evident. The instant we begin to worship, we know that neither our personal capacities nor all the other human beings to whom we are thankful can compose what evokes this response. When a philosophy inevitably suppresses, or fails adequately to express, this sense of thankfulness for mercies unearned and for goods that have been magnified beyond any human devising, then it can be claimed, partly on the basis of psychoanalytic principles themselves, that this philosophy is starving the most potent resource of all for human transformation and beatitude.

CHAPTER VIII

Static Views of Salvation

THEOLOGIANS REGARD THE possibility of bondage to sin as linked with God's purpose in granting men the gift of freedom. There is no way in which even God could create human beings capable of making moral decisions without running the risk that such freedom would be abused. There is no way in which even God could create persons capable of organizing awareness of the universe in terms of value-systems of their own, without running the risk that they would center these systems in themselves instead of in Him. There is no way in which God could make men "like" Himself without running the risk that they would try to "play God." If one asks, in view of the past history and the present prospects of the race, whether it may not be that God's gift of freedom, with these attendant risks, has proved a horrible mistake, the answer depends, in part, on whether one believes that freedom, *with all its attendant evils,* is better than the alternative. The alternative, so far as we can see, would be no human life at all; no risks, no defeats, no triumphs.

Theology also holds, of course, that God possesses inexhaustible resources for dealing with sin, and that the operation of these resources is discernible in two forms. The first is usually called divine "judgment"; it sets limits to the destructiveness of evil, mainly through the tendency of evil to destroy itself. There are minimal principles of order and justice which any individual life and any society must fulfill if they are to be maintained at a human level at all. Men cannot violate these principles with impunity. Whenever they do violate them the outward results are visible as crime, injustice and war; the inward, invisible result is a diseased soul. Even if evil individuals and societies seem to "get away with it," instead of wiping themselves off the map, their rebellion against God turns out to be a hollow victory. They succeed only in depriving themselves of beatitude, and one salient mark of their deprivation may be the fact that they are unaware of their loss. But the limits which divine judgment sets to lawlessness and selfishness should be regarded mainly as necessary expedients for keeping the human enterprise going, in order that a more positive purpose may be served.

God's second strategy in His struggle with man is the redemptive one of actually transmuting evil; both in the individual and in society, He converts anxiety into trust and selfishness into love. Because the first strategy involves holding the effects of sin in check, it may go against the way man tries to employ his freedom. But the second strategy must operate *by means of* his freedom. If the shift from centering the universe in oneself to centering it in God is to be genuine, what occurs must be voluntary, not coerced. Therefore, God's "problem" in redemption is one of winning man out of bondage to self-centeredness into spontaneous affirmation of love as the fulfillment of man's own beatitude.

Christians believe that this redemptive purpose has been revealed supremely in the life and sacrifice of Jesus Christ. He reveals the willingness of God to forgive sinners and to restore them to fellowship with Himself. He reveals the forthgoing, active character of a divine love which does not leave man to writhe in bondage, but takes the initiative in breaking through the spiritual fetters. The life of sacrifice, whereby the Son of God shares our human temptations and limitations, takes upon Himself the burden of our guilt, and prays for the forgiveness of those who slay Him, can break through hard-heartedness and hopelessness, awakening men both to the shamefulness of their selfishness and to the possibility of a new, rectified, transformed existence. He makes us aware of the depth of our shortcomings when we are estranged from God, and of the height of our destiny when we are restored to right relationship with God. The gift which He offers is addressed to our freedom, since response to it involves our decision. Yet it is at the same time designed to break through the defenses of our self-centered wills so as to "capture" them and to awaken love within us—despite our disposition to remain in sin.

Notice how the paradox of bondage and responsibility which we encountered in the preceding chapter is repeated in connection with saving faith. In order to be genuine, this faith must be reached through man's decision; yet God takes the initiative in such a way that the redeemed man feels that he has been captured, despite himself. Only as he surrenders can he "freely" affirm the divine power to which he capitulates. Hence he does not regard the human decision which he contributed as having enabled him to "save himself"; for his beatitude rests not in self-assertion, but in becoming reconciled to God, and in serving Him.

For many Christians one of the most inspiring aspects of this belief has been the realization that a man does not have to undertake the hopeless task of making himself good, by sheer, moralistic will-power, before being able to come into the presence of God trustfully. For them the heart of the Gospel has been the message that God is willing to accept them as they are, if they will turn to Him in penitence and faith. The story of the Prodigal Son illustrates the fact that no "conditions" are attached to reconciliation except that the individual himself shall desire to return to his Father. Yet this divine willingness to forgive does not spring from moral indifference. The suffering of Christ is taken, in various ways, as indicating the costliness of redemption. God takes evil seriously, but He also takes its burden upon Himself, through Christ, in the course of refusing to let it destroy love. Hence all forms of Christian theology regard God as using a strategy higher than "mere" justice in seeking to root out evil at its source. "Mere" justice would lead to a straightforward judgment upon sin. This occurs; but it is not the end of the matter. Faith opens a way whereby sin is not allowed to lead to the otherwise inevitable consequence of exclusion from fellowship with a righteous God; it opens a way whereby we get something better than we deserve.

Any one who has felt his own life relieved of egotism, anxiety and evil-doing through such beliefs, and who in the fellowship of a Christian Church has observed how these same beliefs have molded, strengthened and enriched the lives of others, may think that it is presumptuous to examine them psychologically. We should remember, however, what has happened in the past whenever efforts have been made to safeguard the power and purity of Christian beliefs by walling them off from the influences of natural science and historical criticism. In the end, the Church has had to remove the wall in order to be faithful to her own concern for the truth—or it has compromised with that concern. A conception of God which regards Him as less than the ground of *all* truth is unworthy of our loyalty. And unless we can carry forward any honest line of investigation, with the confidence that what is valid in it is compatible with what is valid in our version of Christianity, we cannot be wholly sincere and unafraid in our religious faith.

Accordingly, let us first recognize that Christian convictions can be so expressed as to attribute salvation *exclusively* to divine action and *not at all* to human response. Berdyaev has declared that this type of theological thinking drove him, for a time, into atheism; and one can see why. God, foreknowing how man will abuse his freedom (don't give this a second thought), also determines in advance who shall be saved and who shall be damned. Why this deterministic view does not make God *wholly* responsible for sin is never satisfactorily explained; the best attempts hold that although God permits the activities of sinful men, our motives in the performance of these activities are culpable, while God permits evil only insofar as it is contributory to the good. In any case, men who are predestined to exclusion from saving faith get punished eternally for not possessing it. How such an outcome fulfills the sovereign will of a loving God is also not explained. Instead, we are told that men have no right to question God's decrees which issue from the unfathomable mystery of His wisdom. But then the theologian proceeds to fathom the mystery, at least to the extent of claiming that no man has any ground for complaint. If he is saved, that is more than he could ever deserve; if he is damned, that is just what he deserves. In the one case God manifests His mercy, in the other case His justice; and He has good reason in both cases, since the objects of the former possess saving faith, while the objects of the latter are unregenerate sinners. If one protests that questions concerning what a man deserves can hardly arise so long as his own volition is powerless to affect the outcome, the reply is that God is running the universe and that man's proper role is to put his fate in God's hands, trusting to His mercy and justice, and believing in the inscrutable rightness of whatever happens.

An account of this extreme theological position has been introduced at this point in order to remind us of how diverse the connotations of "dependence on God," "faith in Christ," "conviction of sin," and "belief in salvation" can be. We should remember, of course, that the notion of divine judgment need not be associated exclusively with vivid pictures of sinners frying in Hell. Many theologians prefer to identify divine judgment primarily with those conditions in man's soul and in his society which keep him estranged from love; and as we look at the world we may feel that this is "punishment" enough. They may further argue that unless there were real possibilities of failure in life, as well as of fulfillment, human decision could make no difference to the sort of person one becomes. In other words, if the reality of freedom is consistent with God's loving purposes, then the consequences of the abuse of that freedom must also be consistent with those purposes. How far such reflections carry one toward a complete answer to the problem of evil is another matter. Obviously they do not cover evils which are not connected with the abuse of human freedom.

Even when they are not associated with an extreme version of the doctrine of predestination, however, Christian conceptions of salvation can take forms which must be regarded from a psychological standpoint as tyrannical. Divine love (*Agape*) is taken as the norm for human life; insofar as a man falls short of it, he is sinful; insofar as it is being fulfilled in him, he is redeemed and tending toward salvation. Yet because Christ is regarded as the only man who ever has or ever could perfectly embody *Agape,* this norm is put beyond the reach of the rest of the race. From such a perspective it is always possible to condemn men for failing to follow Christ; but if they are told that Christ alone could fulfill such perfection anyway, they are hardly to be blamed for thinking that the condemnation is unreasonable. This doctrine scolds them for not being replicas of Christ, and then scolds them if they believe that they could be. Against it we must hold that unless what Christ signifies can be related positively to resources and possibilities which are discoverable in men generally, He cannot open the way to aims and standards they can make their own. In order to be relevant to the recognition of failure and to be effective in guiding toward transformation, a conception of salvation must be related directly to the individual's own insight, motivation and action. Let us grant that he cannot move toward salvation or reach it without divine grace. Nevertheless, the man must embody what happens. It is his conscience, his judgments, his attitudes that get transformed. This transformation occurs, not by abrogation of his human capacities, but through the highest employment of them. If there is nothing in the individual which is akin to Christ, then Christ, as a norm for his life, is simply alien—and powerless.

Another psychological criticism may take the form of claiming that theology has not ordinarily carried far enough its analysis of the implications of man's bondage to sin. This criticism is closely related to the preceding one. If men are so immersed in sin that they are basically at war with the good, then does it not follow that the way in which they conceive of ethical ideals and religious goals is bound to be distorted? Yet many theologians write as though quite indiscriminate acceptance of the obligation to be perfectly loving and self-sacrificial—even when one literally *cannot* fulfill this obligation—were synonymous with a sound, clear-eyed exercise of conscience. They may take acknowledg-

ments of guilt and human impotence as indications of a high
stage of religious insight, when these should be taken as indications of serious unresolved problems. And if the theologian hastily
adds that guilt and impotence *have* been overcome in Christ, it
is entirely legitimate to reply that this avails little unless guilt and
impotence have been overcome in the individual also—not merely
in a theoretical way, but dynamically.

The central question which thus emerges has to do with the
effectiveness of ideal standards. For reasons that will be made
clear as we go along, we shall call the two conflicting answers
to this question "static" and "dynamic." The static view assumes
that ethical and religious progress is most effectively promoted,
and the perils of indifference and irresponsibility are best avoided,
by holding before the eyes of men a vision of perfection which
will keep them perpetually ashamed of themselves. This interpretation of Christianity has often been saved from falling into
sheer moralism by its belief that the ideal for human life (Christ)
has been actualized, and by its belief that this actualization is
accessible to the race by means other than legalistic rigors. Divine
grace, as mediated through faith and the sacraments, is the actualization in man of something he could not achieve by himself.
Nevertheless, a conception of salvation is static so long as it imposes an obligatory pattern without regard to the specific needs
and capacities of the growing and changing individual. It is
static so long as it is employed to measure a man against an
external, pre-established standard, granting approval insofar as
he can squeeze himself into conformity with it and issuing condemnation insofar as he fails to do so. Such a view keeps belief
and conduct at odds with each other; it anticipates and asserts
that man must always fall short of what he "believes." All men
are in the sinful predicament of not being able to do what they
ought, regardless of the vast individual differences between them
in terms of handicaps or assets—physical, mental and cultural.
Man is not expected to be able to make significant inroads on
the power of sin by any positive participation on his own part.
His proper role is to confess and repent. Salvation takes place,

in the first instance, quite outside and apart from the needy individual. Indeed, if he believes that he can make any positive contribution toward it, his failure to acknowledge complete dependence upon God is a sign of pride, an additional indication that he is enslaved to sin.

Perhaps it may seem paradoxical to call such an interpretation of Christianity "static" when it places exclusive stress upon the judging and redeeming *activity* of God. Yet from man's standpoint the situation is static because his norms for living and his salvation are conceived of, not in terms of discoveries and dynamic changes within him, but in terms of an alteration of his status before God—a shift from condemnation to justification in the light of what Christ has done. Even when man responds gratefully and trustfully to this saving work of Christ, he can claim no share in the inward regeneration; that is exclusively God's accomplishment. In fact, the only thing man is responsible for, apparently, is what drives him into sin.

The consequences of this static view of salvation may be manifold, but we shall confine our discussion to a few basic examples that reflect the psychological principles which have been outlined in preceding chapters. The first consequence is hypocrisy. The individual assents (perhaps sincerely) with a part of his mind to belief in Christian salvation, but he lives in a way that does not remotely approximate Christ as the Pattern. His actions and inward attitudes say more eloquently than words ever can that there is no mutually enriching interplay between the norm he assents to and the policies he lives by. Insofar as a man is aware of such hypocrisy either he may be deeply troubled by his failure, or he may find ways of remaining fairly jaunty about it. These opposite reactions lead to other results which we shall examine presently. But in both instances the situation perpetuates conflict. Discrepancies between the professed norm and actual living can be overcome only by so altering one or both of them that they can move toward coincidence with each other. Movement toward such coincidence is impossible, however, so long as clinging to the norm is regarded as wholly good and whatever resists it is regarded as wholly bad. Therefore, from both a religious and a psychological point of view, it is important to challenge the assumption that in this conflict God is exclusively on one side and man exclusively on the other—God on the side of the "perfect" norm and man immersed in the sinful resistance. If the norm is being held in such a way that it involves a repudiation of life-giving, creative factors which are the source of spontaneity and human love, then it is *not* "perfect," and it blocks God's self-impartation to man.

A second possible consequence is self-righteousness. Mere entertainment of a grandiose picture of the "saved" condition may convince the individual that he has reached it. So long as he comfortingly identifies himself with the vision, his sense of exalted worthiness remains undisturbed. A realistic scrutiny of his motives and practices would expose limitations in himself and in the harsh, insensitive world which do not comport well with this vision. Hence, insofar as possible, the person stays within the security of his "dream" and regards himself as too good for this world. Many psychotherapists encounter patients who demand to be judged by their "dreams"; at the core they conceive of themselves as perfect, or nearly so; their "real selves" must be exempted from responsibility for the upsetting or restricting conditions that get in their way. When such a vision of perfection is combined with a metaphysical or theological system that assures them the "real" world already fulfills this vision, they are in a position to discount anything which cuts athwart it as "mere appearance."

A third possible consequence, however, is unresolved despair. Here allegiance to the static norm is combined with a thorough awareness of the shortcomings of the self and society. In agony over human imperfection and sin, one may be driven to put one's hope and confidence exclusively in God. In an important segment of contemporary European Protestantism, such an attitude is regarded as reaching the highest level of Christian insight. In America, where there are so many things we can still do, or at least think we can do, it may be difficult to comprehend the situation of a person whose awareness of impotence and failure seems to coincide closely with the facts. As we toss out strategies through education, psycho-analysis, or anything else, for remedying the evils of our time, we need to ask ourselves how we would go about implementing them if we were living in certain sections of Europe or Asia. The fact remains, however, that despair which completely abandons hope in human, temporal possibilities is *unresolved*. The accompanying trust in God and His unshatterable, supra-historical purposes may be the only thing that prevents the despairing individual from falling into cynicism, insanity or suicide; and where this is the case, one may want to refrain from tampering with it. The question of theological adequacy involves additional considerations, however, which should be dealt with on their own merits. Actually, unless faith in God can direct us to historical possibilities that can be implemented and believed in, important aspects of Christian trust are being omitted. Without some affirmation of human nature (even though this affirmation be confined to whatever it is in men that makes them redeemable), it is impossible for a Christian actively to express what he assents to doctrinally—namely, love for mankind despite its sinfulness. Where such affirmation is completely ruled out of court, on the supposition that faith in God is thereby made pure and absolute, theology becomes an oblique means for expressing self-hatred and hatred for mankind under the guise of saying the opposite. Similarly, where theology completely sunders salvation from resources that are immanent in human nature, it becomes an oblique means for expressing despair over God's impotence in history under the guise of affirming His transcendent sovereignty.

We have been scrutinizing a form of unresolved despair which clings to a static norm. The opposite reaction, of course, leads to an abandonment of the ideal norm, and a cynical or defiant alliance with "unregenerate" human nature. Nietzsche's attack on Christianity typifies this, and we should note in passing the kinship-of-opposition which exists between modern Christian pessimism and modern anti-Christian pessimism. A perfectionist contempt for man underlies both, though it leads to opposite conclusions.*

A fourth possible consequence, though it may be an ingredient in any of the three already mentioned, is extreme self-repudiation. The conscientious and sincere believer comes to regard *every* expression of self-assertion as sinful. To him the literal fulfillment of Christian love involves something similar to self-immolation. His static conception of salvation provides him with no effective means for discriminating between egocentric selfishness and a sound form of self-love. The theological formula which sets love for God in stark opposition to self-love throws no light whatever on the difference between those resistances to self-sacrifice which springs from conceit, cowardice or cynicism, and those which spring from a legitimate desire to live "abundantly." In psychological language, this *way* of espousing Christianity plays directly into masochistic patterns: —endless self-castigation, without *wanting* anything to happen which will remove the sense of being helpless to do the good, plus a sense of coming closest to fulfillment of God's will precisely to the extent that one does not presume to organize his human resources for the maintenance of his own life and his own interests.

Thus we see that retention of an ideal which is forever beyond man's reach does not automatically prevent egotism, complacency and disillusionment. On the contrary, a view of life which concentrates mainly upon shortcomings may drive men into fantasy, or paralyzed hopelessness, or cynical rebellion—or into further desperate efforts which fail to resolve the situation.

*The deprecatory things said about man by Karl Barth and Bertrand Russell are sometimes verbally similar, though in the one case they spring from a "neo-orthodox" theology and in the other case from naturalistic atheism. That both of them are capable, in various ways, of cheerfulness, charitableness and humor, should not surprise us. Men are frequently more sensitive and less consistent than their thinking.

CHAPTER IX

A Dynamic View of Salvation

OVER AGAINST THE foregoing results, let us set a "dynamic" conception of salvation. Here the validity of an ethical or a religious ideal depends upon its power to *resolve* conflict. Insofar as a person finds organic harmony between his ideals and his unforced behavior, the resulting release and serenity provide a firm and stimulating basis for further development along the same lines. He becomes a "gracious" instead of a "moralistic" human being. So far as Christianity is concerned, this conception implies that its saving purpose is to give men a faith and a mode of life which will make them no longer ashamed of themselves. It cures guilt, not by putting forward ideas which assure men willy-nilly that they are "all right," but by releasing a power which removes the *causes* of guilt.

The stock objection is that, if one allows a man to be content with ideals he is actually able to reach, he will "accept himself" at an immoral or complacent level. But the clinical data of psychotherapy point to an opposite conclusion. Most emotional disorders and behavior problems reveal a pattern where the individual has *not* reached self-acceptance—which is functionally interrelated, incidentally, with his capacity to accept others. On the contrary, such personality problems go hand-in-hand with a sense of moral inferiority, unacceptability and estrangement, no matter how much these may be overlaid with a bold, defiant "front." Under present circumstances coercive methods have to be used in protecting society against the consequences that would ensue if moral evil were allowed to run rampant. These coercive methods range from punishment in home and school to imprisonment of criminals and resistance of aggressors in war. But such methods do not "cure" anything. A constructive transformation is not brought about merely by driving home upon either an individual or a nation an acknowledgment of moral inferiority and its consequences. Men can be frightened into abiding by certain restrictions, or otherwise compelled to abide by them; but these expedients do not alter motivation in a desirable direction. Whether we think of domestic crime or of international warfare, who can deny that the threat of punishment and the enforcement of retaliation are staggeringly inefficient as methods of preventing anti-social behavior? Permanent cures occur only insofar as a man finds forms of affection, respect and trust in which he can participate. Such values are "self-sustaining" in the sense that once they are experienced, a man wants them, affirms those things in himself which promote them, and voluntarily renounces those things in himself which would destroy them. Even if most human beings (past and present) are regarded as "incurable" because limitations in themselves or in their surroundings have excluded the fulfillment of these conditions, that does not invalidate the psychological principles involved.

None of this means, however, that an ideal must be *immediately* realizable in order to be dynamic. One can acknowledge the desirability of a style of life, a family relationship, or a social order which neither he nor any one else has yet achieved. He can retain belief in the worth of such ideals despite the fact that they remain in some measure unattainable in any foreseeable future. But his ideals are held in such a way that failure can be made a priceless source of deepening understanding and effective change—instead of a source of paralysis and despair. Admittedly it is exceedingly difficult to discriminate aright between the factors in any human problem that cannot be changed and those which can be. But so long as a norm is employed statically, all failure to fulfill it is condemned forthwith; hence discrimination cannot even get started. In general, most people who are caught in serious conflict blame themselves for things they cannot help, and fail to move toward procedures which are within their power. For example, they scold themselves for an outburst of rage, anxiety or eroticism which, at the existing level of self-understanding, was quite inevitable; but they feel sincerely that they "cannot" face what lies behind their problems.

If an ideal is dynamic, it provides positive guidance concerning the extent to which, and the methods by which, it can be effectively promoted. Insofar as obstacles are strictly irremediable, one operates within the limits they set; one does not cling to a vision of perfection in defiance of them, and one does not blame either himself or any one else for failing to do the impossible. Let us acknowledge again that often the line between the remediable and the irremediable cannot be drawn with certainty. We can be certain that man cannot slough off his body and live as pure spirit, so that any ethic which is applicable only to the latter condition may be disregarded. But we cannot be certain, for example, as to whether a specific endeavor toward lessening racial prejudice will evoke enough of a favorable response to outweigh the hatred it may stir up. The latter dilemma illustrates why well-intentioned persons can differ honestly concerning the best strategy for promoting the same end. It also illustrates why ideal norms should be alterable in the light of continual study of empirical data. A dynamic approach is our best available method for moving flexibly between the Scylla of impractical idealism (which underestimates the odds ranged against it), and the Charybdis of compromising cynicism (which underestimates the releasability of moral resources).

Similarly, in our religious conceptions of salvation there must be organic connection between the goal itself and the human conditions which are to be fulfilled in reaching it. Because the conditions on which human beatitude rests do not consist merely of external techniques and operations, theology must steadily resist those modes of thought which look upon the problem involved merely as a piece of psychological and sociological engineering. The "Brave New World" is a secular substitute for salvation, and many of our contemporaries worship at its shrine, either because they believe it is the best they can get, or because they have become so spiritually obtuse as actually to believe it is splendid. Yet Christianity's purpose of calling men to a higher destiny cannot be served if its manner of "facing the worst" about human nature prevents it from finding realistically and practically those areas in which significant changes are feasible. Where it is literally the case concerning a personal or social problem that nothing can be done about it, the only wise course involves accepting the restriction and focusing attention upon anything that can be accomplished despite its limits. Human beings have amazing capacities for morale and adjustment when they know definitely what they are up against. The circumstances that drive them into despair, insanity and suicide are mainly connected with man-made events. Strictly unpreventable evils can make life tragic; it is the preventable evils *which become* inexorable that make life intolerable.

Hence salvation should be thought of primarily in terms of a dynamic transformation that removes man-made evils at the source by changing the man. It should not be thought of in terms that would require a complete sloughing off of creatureliness. We have already suggested that the Theology of Crisis (in its most extreme version) is wrong when it regards the conditions of salvation as fulfilled exclusively by God, apart from existing resources in human nature. We have also contended that humanism is wrong in claiming that the conditions of salvation (or "amelioration") must be fulfilled exclusively by man, because there is no God. The preceding discussion has led up to a conception of salvation as that condition of wholeness which comes about when human life is based in openness (*i.e.*, with "self-knowledge") upon the creative and redemptive power of God. This condition is reached *by means of* man's freedom, and constitutes an enhancement of that freedom. Its initiation, once or repeatedly, may involve "taking him captive"; but the "captivation" is releasing and the released person affirms it and desires to sustain it. The freedom of man, as we have conceived it, is directly related to acquaintance with his own depths; his assent cannot be unforced and wholehearted if it is opposed by unconscious motives and impulses. Yet the very process of widening acquaintance with the sources of human bondage leads to the release of healing power. In other words, the structure of reality links misery and conflict to man's failure to reach a position where he can affirm his *whole* self; and it links beatitude to honesty and wholeness. Hence faith in God can rest upon actualities that function in human existence here and now; it need not be directed exclusively to something which utterly transcends our experience and our history.

In theological language, our conception of salvation definitely involves acceptance of the doctrine of divine immanence.* The drive toward integration, which man can discern in himself, is not confined to him. It moves through all levels of creation; but in man the problem of how to reach integration-in-freedom gives rise to unparalleled difficulties and opportunities. Man's freedom shuts him off from reaching harmony by becoming an item in the routine and vitality of natural process—a harmony which animals enjoy. But it is equally impossible for man to reach wholeness by attempting to fulfill "divine" demands which transcend his status as a temporal creature in nature. The principles whereby man reaches harmony within himself are at once rational and "animal," spiritual and physical. The destiny of man cannot be conceived apart from his linkage with processes at every level in nature. In this sense God moves *through* His creation. As Fritz Kunkel has put it: "Creation continues." Moreover, the doctrine of the Resurrection issues from a (Jewish) view of man's psycho-physical wholeness which is congenial with the foregoing, while Platonic views of immortality are incompatible with it.

The identification of "the voice of conscience" with "the voice of God" leads to a dangerous half-truth so long as the voice of conscience perpetuates conflict instead of resolving it. As Berdyaev has suggested, the Gospel is "strange" not merely because it comes to us over a chasm of twenty centuries; it is "strange" because it is anti-legalistic. It is personal, whereas every culture's

---

*I am concerned to stress this point because this doctrine has been strenuously attacked by Barthian theology. Affirmation of divine immanence does not here imply a denial of divine transcendence.

moral ideas—whether those of the first century or the twentieth century—tend to be collective and tyrannical. The relationship to God it envisages is spontaneous, whereas all ethical *law* is abstract and compulsive. If he is right, then the voice of God speaks and the creative power of God moves through forms of organic solidarity with nature and with fellow human beings which the condemning conscience rejects. Both moralism and rationalism, insofar as they estrange man from parts of himself, prevent him from reaching wholeness. And a theology that denies or minimizes the immanence of God cannot use the full resources of the Gospel in counteracting the distortions of human nature which result.

We have already rejected the theory of revelation which regards man's likeness to God as so completely destroyed that nothing in him can participate in the achievement of salvation. We have also rejected views of salvation through Christ which impose upon men a norm they are not expected to appropriate through their own insight and through the emancipating consequences that flow from insight. Belief in Christ is compatible with a dynamic view of salvation, however, when it finds in Him the supreme disclosure of a universal fact—the fact that divine and human love cannot be fulfilled apart from each other. In such a conception His union with God is not used tyrannically as the basis for condemning other men because they are incapable of reproducing His unique endowments. Instead, He points to the redeemability of *our* human nature, and to the possibility of reaching self-acceptance in fellowship with God.

In the process of reaching maturity and autonomy most of us do strive for security by trying to organize the universe around ourselves. And most of us learn only through the suffering and estrangement which attend egocentricity that this way leads not to security, but to an endlessly precarious and ultimately fruitless attempt to twist reality into meeting our private specifications. Insofar as we are incapable of love, we are not only divided within ourselves and isolated from other human beings, we are violating the universal principle upon which human beatitude is based. Our defensive structures are broken through by healing power which is wider than ourselves; yet it is ours. We see—not merely intellectually, but with heart and soul—that what is made accessible to us in our "new" selves has been what we have yearned for all along. We have evaded it partly because the price in suffering seemed too high, especially when there was no guarantee of a satisfying outcome. We have also "evaded" it because we literally could not work toward it effectively so long as we were imprisoned within the old strategies of defensiveness, anxiety and the need to feel superior. The price in suffering is a facing and grasping, in feeling as well as in thought, of the deeply hidden causes of inner dividedness. This facing can be carried on healingly (*i.e.*, redemptively) only in a relationship of acceptance (*i.e.*, forgiveness).

We reach our highest freedom not by asserting our own interests against the world, but by devoting ourselves in fellowship to a way of life which reaches personal fulfillment along with, and partly *through,* the fulfillment of others. We reach security only by a trustful acceptance of the full truth about ourselves and others, not by evasion of it. Healing power is latent in men because it is latent "in the nature of things." Hence it is not surprising that men and women have found in Christ the supreme disclosure of what coincidence between human beatitude and divine love means. Christ is Savior as He opens, for each man, the way whereby that individual can move toward such coincidence. This involves moving forward into a deepened recognition of failure, impotence and need at many points. But the divine forgiveness which He discloses always has been and always will be accessible to men. We experience divine forgiveness as that "making right" of our lives which occurs when we turn away from fighting ourselves, and others, and the truth itself, and turn trustfully toward the divine power which surrounds us and can work through us. This experience of reconciliation, despite past failures and unsolved problems in the present, makes men actually more lovable, more discerning, more capable of devoting themselves to goods which enrich all humanity.

Christian theology impoverishes itself, however, when it conceives of divine love (*Agape*) and human love (*Eros*) as opposed to each other.* There is a direct connection between suitable "erotic" expression and a man's capacity for Christian "charity." Strained attempts to conquer egotism and to reach selfless devotion to God often end in failure because of a "conscientious" mishandling of the bodily springs of human affection. It is no accident when ascetic saints find it impossible to put warmth into the neighbor-love of which the Gospel speaks. It is no accident when they are confronted, from time to time, with disturbing visions welling up from the unconscious. Such visions are not followed out in practice, and they loom up only when the individual's source of conscious control is in abeyance. Yet they are symptomatic of hidden parts of his character-structure which influence everything he thinks, feels and does. To be sure, sexual needs can be so completely sublimated that some ascetics are capable of enviable generosity and serenity. However, where there is a starved body there is, at some level, an angry man; and often the strains which cause the buried hostility go hand-in-hand with the extraordinary disciplinary measures that are used to keep it in check. In any case, we must deny that the "love" which fulfills God's purposes for human life is approximated or reached only through rejection of *Eros*. On the contrary, *Eros* is an integral part of what human wholeness means.

Yet in the history of theology specific discussions of sex have fallen prevailingly under the topic "sin" and have received scant positive attention under the topic "salvation." The desirability of subordinating sexual interests by means of ethical and spiritual restraints has enjoyed extensive, though not necessarily sound, treatment. Sexuality has been regarded usually as something which gets spoiled by sinfulness, instead of as being intrinsically sinful; yet the major portion of the Church's interest has always been directed toward ways and means of holding the erotic down.

*The latter term connotes the whole range of human affection; it should not be narrowly confined to sex, although our discussion at this point must devote major attention to sexual implications.

Little has been said concerning the positive contribution it can make to "the good life" as a partner instead of as a treacherous servant.

Undeniably there are situations where there is no middle ground between (a) sexual expression which would plunge the individual into tragedy, and (b) total sublimation or repression. Homosexuality is a notable example. Moreover, the tragedies connected with the first alternative must not be underestimated: paralyzing guilt, break-up of homes, social ostracism. But the Church has prevailingly supported the most exacting standards as unalterable, and placed the whole load of adjustment upon the individual.

Christian salvation cannot be conceived in such a way that it incorporates what would make each man whole unless theology pays more attention than it has in the past to the widely divergent needs and capacities of different individuals. (1) For many persons in our competitive culture the chief problem is connected with their aggressive, egocentric fixation upon material possessions, social-standing and power, and with their starvation of those resources which make for sympathy, affection and friendship (free from "calculation"). (2) At the opposite pole, however, the chief problem can be connected with slavish dependence, lack of firmness, and a symbiotic living through others. This can take forms which look like laudable Christian meekness; but it is uniformly accompanied by unconscious self-seeking and hostility. An extreme version of it is known as the martyr-complex. The remedy, in this second case, involves not an increase in "self-sacrifice," but an increased outlet for open, responsible forms of self-maintenance which can replace unrecognized, disguised forms of resentment. (3) For some, the chief problem is connected with aloofness and with fear of being entangled in any sort of give-and-take relationship. (4) For others, a perpetual need for companionship indicates failure to achieve enough self-possession so that one can stand it to be alone. Hence the blanket formulæ whereby theology has customarily defined sin in terms of egocentricity and salvation in terms of self-sacrifice need to be modified in the light of psychological information concerning the varieties of human temperament and character.

In *Man for Himself,* Erich Fromm has shown that the equation between self-love and egocentricity is misleading. Our capacity to love others is, as he puts it, "conjunctive with" our capacity to love humanity in our own persons. Dr. Fromm does not believe in God. Nevertheless, theology can carry his principle a stage further and hold that capacity to respond to God's love is directly related to self-love (self-acceptance). As is clear from the foregoing chapters, I do not believe that man can reach self-acceptance "all by himself." The power which emancipates him from enslavement to a bad conscience is divine as well as human. But the end result of such emancipation is not love for God and hatred for self; it is affirmation of self as grounded in God. Since no man can know perfectly and finally the extent to which his life fulfills this affinity, the danger of self-deification is omnipresent and if the individual were confined to his own unaided powers he would be at the mercy of the danger. But life does not leave him shut up to his own powers. Or, rather, we should note that such shut-upness, such inability to differentiate between oneself and God, when it does occur, constitutes insanity. Even though we cannot employ it infallibly, however, our guiding concept measures salvation not by self-repudiation, but by fruition and joy.

Christian salvation is constituted by trust in God, inward harmony, and the interpersonal relations which accompany such a condition. Recognition of identity between the redemptive power which is operative in life, and what Christ stands for, will lead to assent to the doctrine that He is the Savior of mankind. But salvation is not equatable with assent to *any* doctrine. We are saved through being enabled to bring our selves, with their possibilities and limitations, into the service of the redemptive power which Christ incarnates. We are not saved through trying to eradicate our selves and live through Christ as a substitute.

Therefore the utmost importance attaches to the way in which a believer seeks to "follow Christ," especially with regard to suffering. "Willingness to sacrifice," when exalted indiscriminately as synonymous with the Christian way of life, exposes theology to various forms of confusion. It gives masochistic people good grounds for believing that they are the "best" Christians; and it baffles sincerely religious people who find themselves inevitably balking at the "demands" of the Gospel. Whether sacrifice is a supreme manifestation of goodness depends on the manner in which the individual enters into it, and upon its connection with his ideals and his love. It can be, and often is, a means of expressing self-hatred in the form of self-punishment. One "gives himself a beating" by rigorously imposing self-denial. But this expedient seldom, if ever, removes the *cause* of guilt by effectively altering the recalcitrant motives or the perfectionist fixations which keep one mired in guilt. Instead of being irrefutable evidence that a saving transformation has occurred, extreme forms of self-denial may be the sign of failure to begin the transformation which is most needed. Refusal to sacrifice may be due, of course, to simple selfishness; but the sacrifice cannot be an expression of spiritual health until selfishness has been dealt with at the core. Selfishness cannot be removed by an act which "looks like" altruism or penance. That is why Protestantism is right when it insists that "good works" can flow from an internal transformation, but that they cannot produce it.

Refusal to sacrifice may also be due, however, to a legitimate concern for one's own welfare and the welfare of others, which will be violated if one simply gives way. If love involves caring about the promotion of responsible freedom in other men, then it is not a manifestation of "love" to let them get away with murder, either literally or figuratively speaking. Indeed, it is often quite compatible with love to let an infantile or tyrannical person come up against the full inconvenience of the consequences of his childishness or cruelty. Here the motive and aim are determinative. If the motive is one of setting my will-to-power against his, in order to demonstrate that I am stronger, or if it is one of hatred sent forth to meet hatred, then obviously the "hard-boiled" treatment is not loving. But justice is compatible with love so long as it is aimed at safeguarding the welfare of others and of oneself; both can be directed toward helping the infantile person to grow up, or toward providing the tyrannical person with stimuli for revising his tactics.*

Kierkegaard was right in insisting that Christian suffering is to be distinguished from misfortune by the fact that it is *voluntary*. As he suggested, we should not confuse losing one's shirt on the stock exchange with giving one's goods to feed the poor —though the bank-balance may turn out to be the same in both instances. But to agree that Christian suffering is voluntary does not mean that the Gospel bids us run out in search of self-torment; instead, suffering is encountered and accepted in connection with fidelity to aims that we whole-heartedly espouse. As Christians we believe that pain is an evil, all other things being equal; and we seek to reduce it in our own lives as well as in the lives of others. But no one can live long without confronting the fact that love and suffering go together. Christ accepted suffering when the alternative would have been infidelity to His mission; but He did not run after it; He prayed that the cup might pass from Him. And all of us encounter circumstances where *not* to be vulnerable to suffering would mean, quite simply, that we did not care. One does not have to undergo shattering personal tragedies to verify this. Any man alive needs only enough imagination to realize what is happening to the race.

Christ incorporates a universal fact of human existence, then, when He embodies the inescapable connection between suffering and love; and He also discloses the bearing of faith in God upon the way in which we cope with whatever suffering may befall us. For one who does not believe in God, the only sufferings that are alterable are those we unnecessarily cause ourselves. We should not minimize the tremendous relief and enrichment that

*These instances of coincidence between justice and love are not intended to conceal the fact that often, in political decisions especially, a line of action directed toward "the most we can hope for" in the way of justice involves coercive methods that cannot be combined emotionally with love.

can be associated with the removal of these remediable causes of suffering. For the rest, however, which are due to circumstances we are powerless to alter, the man who does not believe in God can do no more than meet them as bravely as possible and wring from them any modicum of good they can be forced to yield. Christian faith does not leave man thus alone in his agony. Instead of regarding the retention of tragic dignity and Stoic firmness as the highest point man can reach in an inward triumph over fate, it sees in man's capacity to make suffering serve love the very center of his communion with God. Christian faith does not "protect" or "exempt" the believer from the common lot of humanity—peril, injury, disease, grief and death. No theodicy, by waving a magic wand, can get rid of a single evil. But the kind of security and beatitude one can reach in life is directly related to whether the linkage between suffering and love is regarded as a brute fact or as a means to fellowship with a suffering, loving God.

Psychotherapy has plunged deeply into the way in which grief, remorse and tragedy can be made to serve sympathy and self-understanding. It knows much about the difference between bondage to fate, suffered in isolation, and serenity reached on the other side of a *shared* facing of misery and terror. Consequently from a Christian perspective its observations concerning what works healingly in men are congruent with belief in God's redemptive working through men. Yet the idea that universally valid principles of life could be supremely manifest in one Person strikes many therapists, as it does many contemporaries generally, as arbitrary. In a sense, of course, all historical events are arbitrary. There is no way of deducing a concrete event or an individual person from the interplay of ideas and essences. If universally valid principles of life are actualized at all, they are actualized in persons. Yet the arbitrariness, in the case of Christian convictions concerning the Person of Christ, seems to go further. The protest against it insists that we must confront our problems in the light of our age, our limitations, our knowledge of human possibilities; and each individual must learn how to confront his problems for himself. The life of a man who lived in Palestine almost two thousand years ago cannot constitute "the final solution." It is bound to contain anachronisms; it is rooted in local ideas and situations which are inapplicable to us; and looking to Him as the final solution diverts us from the necessary task of finding out for ourselves what is highest and best.

Our answer is that whatever is valid in Christ's disclosure of God is universally operative in human life, and, therefore, is verifiable within experience. In order for Christian faith to be genuine, a man must make his own way to the criteria by which he conceives of human beatitude. He will of course make "his own" way in interaction with all the beliefs, Christian and non-Christian, to which he is exposed; and the way that he follows may reflect failure to deal adequately with intellectual, moral or spiritual problems instead of skill in doing so. Nevertheless the appeal, in our claims for Christ, should be to something that is going on, or can go on, in the life of the individual and the community because it is universally human. The movement of thought should be from the operation of healing power in life —love replacing egotism and inward harmony replacing conflict—to a resulting formulation of belief in doctrine. An attempt to reverse the process, to force experience into the confirmation of doctrine, shows a lack of confidence in the power of the Gospel to illuminate, persuade and convert men.

It is difficult to read the New Testament without feeling that the main cause of antagonism or indifference toward it, where these occur, is traceable to ancient controversies and present prejudices (both inside and outside the Church) which get in the way of letting it make its own appeal. If allowed to ponder their gropings toward inclusive understanding of human good, many of our contemporaries might still fall far short of discovering complete coincidence between their own beliefs and the Gospel. What theologian can claim to have reached such coincidence? Nevertheless, the *existing* coincidence in minds alienated from the Church is often much greater than they realize; they are prevented from finding their own judgments and experiences widened and deepened by the New Testament because they are repelled in advance—not by Christ, but by Christians.

Theology has always sought to express doctrinally this linkage between Christ and the universally human, but it has often been fearful of following through the implications. We should expect parallels or approximations to what we find in Christ in the other religions of the world, instead of deprecating them or explaining them away. It is folly to belittle the heroism, love and loyalty men have manifested quite apart from any knowledge of or conscious devotion to Jesus Christ. It is folly to assert that the relationship between "natural" human goodness and "Christian" goodness can only be the negative one of contrast, instead of the positive one of kinship.

Where the question is not one of minimal kinship but of highest fruition, theology has often made the mistake of defining the "highest" as something completely out of reach. Actually its norm can be "highest" only if it points toward the release of personal and social resources for reaching possibilities—not impossibilities. Its highest norm is actualized reconciliation between God and man. This is what Christ means. Because this reconciliation is not static, the distinction between the "natural" and the "redeemed" man can be treacherous. Dogmas may stand still, but personal relationships never do. The universal redemptive power which is struggling with sin and evil *links* Christians with the destiny of mankind; it does not separate them off from the rest of the race. The Christian Church cannot be itself except as it seeks to become *the* human community—and that involves reaching men wherever they are. If God has, in fact, never "let go" of them, then He works through all history, even though the manner of His working is uniquely disclosed and fulfilled in Jesus Christ.

CHAPTER X

Psychology and Theology

OUR FINAL TASK is to consider, more systematically and theoretically than we have done heretofore, the relations between psychology and Christian theology. Those who claim that psychological investigation can, of itself, determine the truth or falsity of religious beliefs usually take it for granted that once the human sources of religion have been brought to light further explanations are superfluous. The psychologist does not deal with anything which goes beyond a natural explanation of human experience and behavior; therefore his integrity as a scientist seems to commit him to the conclusion that all divine beings, from the superstitions of primitive man up to, and including, the Christian God, are figments of human imagination. Accordingly, the psychology of religion becomes the study of how man makes God in his own image.

Against such a perspective we must recall that a psychological account of *all* beliefs and theories is possible in principle. Emotional needs, family influences, rationalizations, superiority and inferiority feelings, and anxieties are just as accessible to investigation in the case of atheists and skeptics as they are in the case of "believers." True opinions enter just as much into the nexus of character-structure as false opinions; granted sufficient information and expertness, one could give a psychological explanation of how a person came to espouse either sort of opinion. Therefore, what differentiates a true position from a false one can never be discovered so long as the search remains solely within the plane of psychological conditions.

The distinction involved at this point is between (a) giving a genetic account of how an idea arises and develops, and (b)

144

passing judgment on its validity. All ideas are psychologically and culturally conditioned, and if we could arrive at truth only by magically insulating ourselves against such conditioning we would be foredoomed to permanent failure; the possibility of scientific knowledge, and all other forms of knowledge, would be destroyed. Therefore, when we assert that a proposition is true, what we must mean is that an appropriate relationship has been established between (a) psychological process and (b) what it apprehends. Of course we cannot deny that there is an intimate connection between the way a mind works, psychologically speaking, and the likelihood of its reaching truth of any kind; but this intimate connection should not blind us to the importance of the distinction just made.

From this it follows that the truth or falsity of a religious belief is never *merely* a psychological question, although psychological considerations are relevant to it. In the end one can pass judgments concerning the validity of a particular belief in God, or belief in God generally, only on the basis of a world-view which purports to incorporate the truth with regard to theological questions. If this world-view denies the reality of God, one can seek to show the compatibility between his own (negative) theological conclusions and the available psychological evidence, but one cannot claim that the validity of his conclusions rests on the latter alone. One of Freud's mistakes, in *The Future of an Illusion,* was to assume that his psychological account of religion in itself justified his philosophical (and theologically negative) position concerning illusion and reality.

Instead of falling into Freud's mistake, many writers have held that, for the sake of its own integrity as a science, psychology must suspend judgment on philosophical and theological issues. In the first chapter of *The Varieties of Religious Experience* William James takes pains to point out that, although certain religious experiences may be pathological, or closely related with sex, fear and morbidity, this does not explain them away. He suggests that a factual account of the mental history of a mystic cannot be decisive for judging the spiritual value of his experiences, and he acknowledges that all states of mind, including scientific theories, are, as he puts it, "organically" conditioned. J. B. Pratt expresses a similar standpoint in *The Religious Consciousness*. He holds that as a psychologist one must look upon religion as a product and instrument of human needs. From this functional point of view, the existence and importance of religion can be acknowledged without raising theological questions; but this does not mean that the latter are illegitimate or superfluous.

We must agree with the two writers just mentioned in acknowledging the distinction between psychological and theological questions. Yet since they carried on their pioneer work in the psychology of religion, it has become increasingly obvious that the problems involved cannot be solved merely by keeping psychology and theology in separate compartments. Theoretically it should be possible for the theologian to incorporate the psychiatric considerations brought forward in this book within his own doctrine of human nature, and it should be possible for the psychiatrist to regard theological questions as outside the scope of his task. But, as we have seen, this division of labor breaks down in practice. The psychiatrist must enter into the realm of theology at least to the extent of asking whether religious beliefs (in any particular case, or perhaps in every case) are illusory; and the theologian can hardly incorporate psychiatric views within his own doctrine of man if the two are radically incompatible with each other.

Since every one faces theological questions in one way or another, how he decides them will have a profound bearing upon his interpretation of the meaning of the psychological facts. Our normative criteria concerning what is good and bad for man, both psychologically and ethically, cannot be divorced from our world-views concerning "man's place in the cosmos." Let us agree that in the long run man is best off insofar as he learns and faces the truth. In special emergency situations there may be certain benefits to be derived from keeping a shaky person intact by leaving his illusions intact. But ultimately there is no sense in trying to make life more secure or more meaningful than it actually is by holding together a set of invalid religious beliefs. If naturalistic humanism is right, man must look solely to himself for the furtherance of ethical principles and for communal endeavors worthy of his loyalty; and the sooner he finds this out, the better. On the other hand, if Christianity is right, then human beatitude is dependent upon an alignment between man's own resources and divine power; and the sooner we learn this, and come to terms with its implications, the better. But it is impossible to settle an issue of this kind by staying within the confines of a purely psychological method. The same facts concerning natural processes and human history can be set into either context; selection of context is determined by a man's "whole response" on religious questions. It is as misleading to say that these empirical facts *prove* the validity of naturalism (in abstraction from personal commitment on religious questions) as to say that they *prove* the existence of God. Therefore, the psychologist who tries to close his eyes to questions of theological validity is forced to indulge in a sort of pretense which distorts the data he is attempting to study. The fetish of "objectivity" compels him to put aside those convictions and attitudes of his own which provide the best possible basis for understanding the religious convictions and attitudes of men generally. As we have already acknowledged, the spectator attitude of science is provisionally useful and justifiable; but the value of scientific truth cannot be isolated from other values. In the last analysis, if a naturalistic theology is to be held against Christian belief in God, it should be based on religious commitment, not on the assumption that one can have insight into such questions best by abstracting himself, so far as possible, from religious concern. In the last analysis we cannot seek to interpret what psychological facts mean, in the sphere of religion, except by employing positive or negative theological convictions. If a religious experience actually is evoked by God, then it is difficult to see what can be gained by treating it as though it were not. And if God is unreal, then this consideration determines the true significance of the phenomena studied by the psychology of religion and provides the indispensable basis for their full explanation.

The foregoing warning against "psychologism" must be coupled, however, with a warning against "theologism." The task of formulating a theological interpretation of man must be tackled afresh in each generation, and what one attempts to say from a Christian perspective can hardly be related effectively to the thought of this generation if it ignores or fails to comprehend the recent contributions which have been made to a "science of man." The task of understanding and ministering to the world's needs is not served wisely by setting up some exclusively theological source of information, and then using it rigidly as a principle of selection in determining what one will welcome or what one will repudiate among the findings of recent psychology. Far too many theological books on the doctrine of man pay lip-service, in passing, to the principle that they have no quarrel with science, and then hasten forward to the exposition of views which have been reached without any serious effort to take account of what psychology, anthropology and sociology have actually contributed. They are written as though God's creative and redemptive activity provides us with a conception of human beatitude into which all empirical information can be deposited, without considering the obverse question as to whether empirical studies of man's capacities, needs and limitations might throw light upon the meaning of sin and salvation.

If there is to be fruitful interplay in these matters, the theologian must be willing to rethink his position in connection with what these sciences of man are uncovering. Indeed, his interpretation cannot be comprehensively true unless it can incorporate whatever they rightly discern. And he can hardly be in a position to draw the important line between where psychologists are staying within the confines of empirical evidence and where they are passing over into theological presuppositions, unless he takes the trouble to consider carefully their most recent methods and findings.

So far as the present situation is concerned, we cannot look to Protestant Fundamentalism or to Roman Catholicism for a contribution because neither is disposed to rethink its theological position. The former tends to be suspicious of science in all forms, and the latter, while capable of granting a limited autonomy to both scientific and philosophical investigations, espouses a view of theological truth which ostensibly puts it beyond the need for reformulation in the light of such inquiries. Yet in those Protestant circles where theologians are free from such disabilities, recent developments have tended to drive Christian belief and the sciences of man farther apart instead of drawing them together. The position that psychology and theology are distinct disciplines, each possessing its own criteria and methods, but capable of co-operation, has been undermined from two directions. One group has been so anxious to bring religious thought into line with science that it has virtually abandoned extra-scientific sources of insight. It has produced valuable studies of religion, drawing heavily upon psychology and anthropology; but either it has deprecated the need for personal faith, or the faith which it has adopted has turned out to be indistinguishable from naturalistic humanism.

The other group takes Christian revelation ("the Word of God speaking through the Bible") as its sole criterion, and sets this criterion in sharp opposition to *all* "merely human" modes of thinking—scientific, ethical and philosophical. It has produced a formidable movement and an increasingly elaborate theology, derived from "the real meaning of the New Testament" and "the real meaning of the Reformation." Having its origin in Europe between two wars, and now occupying a dominant position in Continental Protestantism, this movement—despite internal disagreements—reflects a general revulsion against the modern assumption that man can and need find nothing better than himself and his own cultural aims to worship. Its leaders were face to face with Nazism, and they saw in that phenomenon the logical outcome of an ideology which regards man as a law unto himself—that is, as not subject to principles of justice grounded in the will of God, and not restrained by the respect and love which are due men because of their creation in the image of God. The two major resources whereby modern man has promised himself that he would master the globe and bring in an era of freedom and enlightenment have been science and humanism. But the end result of such an outlook, as these theologians saw it, was the slavery of totalitarianism wherein technological power and all agencies of law, education and enlightenment are pressed into the service of an idolatrous worship of the state, the culture and its *Führer*. The words of Luther: "Man must worship either God or an idol," took on a new meaning. And there can be no question about the fact that this "Theology of Crisis" gave its adherents, during the darkness of the last twenty years, an unrivaled fortitude and boldness in the face of persecution, cynical moral relativism and spiritual disintegration. Despite an increasingly hopeless political prospect, and despite the war and its aftermath—the physical and psychological impact of which few Americans, other than combat troops, can appreciate—these Christian believers were able to retain their faith in God, His sovereign judgments upon human evil and His power to redeem history from the wreckage. Under such circumstances it is not surprising that this theology is severe in its condemnation, not only of modern humanism, but of that form of liberal Protestantism which was popular on the European Continent up through the First World War, and which is still prominent in America. Such liberalism seems to underestimate the seriousness of man's predicament and the potency of his individual and collective sinfulness. By putting its trust in the perfectibility of the human race through science, education, progress and "sweetness and light," it results in a mentality that lacks spiritual fiber—a mentality that is easily overwhelmed by the fanatical and resolute ruthlessness of the totalitarian man. The only remedy for America, as for Europe, according to these theologians, is to recover a Christian faith which can resist political and cultural pressures by refusing to identify human aims (which always reflect sinfulness) with the will of God.

This theological movement has constituted a major revolution in Protestant thought, and even those who are partly or wholly repelled by it cannot understand the contemporary religious situation without taking it into account. Yet the movement has tended to shut off instead of to facilitate collaboration between theology and science. It does not deny the validity of science and philosophy; but within the sphere of theology, it sets up an absolute distinction (one might even say, an absolute opposition) between divine revelation and all human thinking, aspiration or piety.

Within the Theology of Crisis there have been divergent attitudes toward the secular world. The extreme position, represented by Karl Barth, holds that because man, through sin, has utterly lost his capacity to respond to God, one must expect outright opposition to the Gospel. There is no hope whatever of trying to gain converts by finding as much common ground as possible with their secular philosophy, showing the reasonableness of Christianity, and then—after having lured the pagans along this ethical, theistic route—giving them a little shove which will send them over into full-fledged Christian faith. There is head-on collision between the Word of God and the whole pattern of life in this world, and the only honest course for the theologian is to promote the full impact of that collision. He places his confidence in God's power to recreate (regenerate) and redeem man, not in man's natural or latent power to respond to Christ.

A less extreme position, represented by Emil Brunner, has attempted to keep the doors open for discussion between Christians and non-Christians, but it is a one-way passage. In the face of attacks from Barth, Brunner has been anxious to show that everything essential to his position derives from revelation; his "break" with Barth comes at that point where Brunner insists that there remain in man's rational, ethical and religious capacities, despite sin, factors which enable him to respond to the Gospel and confirm it. Hence what Brunner's concessions to "natural" man and "natural" theology amount to is that he sees elements in them that are redeemable; he does not claim that they can contribute positively to the content and activity of redemption itself; this remains, in his theology as in Barth's, wholly God's doing, through Christ. Therefore, beneath the desire to mediate between Christian faith and secular culture, Brunner's thought retains a strongly polemical note, even though it is not so strident as Barth's. Both tend to put the blame for any resistance to their teachings upon the blindness, superficiality, pride and sin of their opponents, and fail to place a sufficient share of the blame upon the prolixity, rigidity, special-pleading and defensiveness of theologians themselves.

Obviously the chasm between this sort of theology and contemporary secular thought in America is terribly wide. Often we must have sympathy with the theologian who has, so to speak, two audiences; first, those who by reason of established familiarity with Christian sources can start from within his basic frame of reference; second, those whose every attitude and idea, because of complete lack of any first-hand appreciation for the meaning of Christian faith, are estranged from the outset from what the theologian is trying to say. We can find a remote parallel for this sort of dilemma in the position of the college professor of American history who finds that half his class has never been exposed to the subject in elementary and secondary education. Nevertheless, the foregoing chapters have made it obvious why, in my opinion, the *way* in which people come into an affirmation of Christian faith is bound to be defective when it occurs in response to a strategy like that of the Theology of Crisis.

The contrasting dangers of "psychologism" and "theologism" arise from contrasting types of abstraction. It is only provisionally, and for the sake of a special purpose, that the psychological conditions of an individual, or of any number of men, can be studied apart from the ultimate philosophical and theological questions which have to do with the structure of reality. It is only provisionally, and for the sake of a special purpose, that the divine source of revelation can be referred to apart from the human conditions under which revelation is received. The two enterprises can be rescued from abstractness only by a continual return to the "I—Thou" relationship. Granted equivalence of psychological knowledge and expertness between two therapists, one who has personally entered into Christian faith is in a more favorable position to interpret the relationship between religious experience and God than one who has not. But even in the latter case, it is personal struggle with questions which transcend psychological data that provides the indispensable basis for understanding religious relationships as one encounters them in others. So far as the theologian is concerned, the most important point to emphasize at the end of our inquiry is the distinction between *reducing* his subject-matter to psychological data and *relating* it to them. As a corrective against the former, the Theology of Crisis has exerted a salutary influence; but the desire to find a basis for making statements about divine revelation which will not be affected by the facts of psychological and cultural conditioning (though the occurrence of such conditioning is not denied) has been carried to illegitimate lengths. Granting that the primary data of theology are not merely psychological phenomena, it is only a professionally acquired blindness to the concrete conditions and limitations of human existence, including the existence of the Church, which prompts the theologian to forget that examination of the human pole of the "I-Thou" relationship is an integral part of his task.

In this book I have attempted to show that some of the basic concepts of psychotherapy are correlative with the human side of events which Christian doctrine interprets. Insofar as I have succeeded it follows that the therapist's description of bondage to inner conflict should be incorporated in the doctrine of sin, and his description of healing (through the release of involuntary changes which occur in a personal relationship of trust and acceptance) should be incorporated in the doctrine of grace. It also follows that ultimately psychiatry cannot understand its own task aright except within the framework of a Christian view of man and God. But the full confirmation of such a standpoint will be reached, if it ever is, only as psychiatrists, and especially Christian psychiatrists, pay more attention than they have thus far to the full range of religious living and faith on the part of strong, healthy people; and it will be reached only as doctrinal theologians take a more direct part in revitalizing the healing ministry of the Church.

SUGGESTIONS FOR FURTHER READING.
Compiled for this edition by Charles R. Stinnette, Jr.

1. In the field of Psychotherapy:

   Sigmund Freud, *Delusion and Dream,* George Allen and Unwin, Ltd., London, 1917.

   Sigmund Freud, "The Dynamics of the Transference," *Collected Papers,* Vol. II, Hogarth Press, London, 1912.

   Sigmund Freud, "The Method of Interpreting Dreams," *The Interpretation of Dreams,* Basic Books, New York, 1958.

   Sigmund Freud, *An Outline of Psychoanalysis,* W. W. Norton, New York, 1949.

   Erich Fromm, *Man for Himself,* Rinehart, New York, 1947.

   Freida Fromm-Reichmann, *Principles of Intensive Psychotherapy,* University of Chicago Press, Chicago, 1950.

   Karen Horney, *Our Inner Conflicts,* Norton, New York, 1945.

   Karen Horney, *Neurosis and Human Growth* (The Struggle toward Self-Realization), Norton, New York, 1950.

   Carl Jung, *The Basic Writings* ed. by Staub De Laszlo, The Modern Library, New York, 1959.

   Karl Menninger, *Theory of Psychoanalytic Technique,* Basic Books, New York, 1958.

   Patrick Mullahy, *Oedipus Myth and Complex* (paperback), Grove Press, New York, 1955.

   Ruth L. Munroe, *Schools of Psychoanalytic Thought,* The Dryden Press, New York, 1955.

   Ira Progoff, *The Death and Rebirth of Psychology,* Julian Press, New York, 1956.

   Carl Rogers, *Client Centered Therapy,* Houghton Mifflin Company, Boston, 1951.

2. In the field of Christian Theology:

   N. Berdyaev, *The Destiny of Man,* Scribner's, New York, 1937.

   N. Berdyaev, *Slavery and Freedom,* Scribner's, New York, 1944.

Emil Brunner, Dogmatics Vol. II *Creation and Redemption,* The Westminster Press, Philadelphia, 1952.

Seward Hiltner, *Preface to Pastoral Theology,* Abingdon, New York, 1958.

Reinhold Niebuhr, *The Nature and Destiny of Man,* 2 vols., Scribner's, New York, 1941 and 1943. (Now available in one volume.)

William Temple, *Nature, Man and God,* Macmillan, New York, 1935.

Paul Tillich, *Systematic Theology,* Vol. I, University of Chicago Press, 1951.

Paul Tillich, *The Courage To Be,* Yale University Press, New Haven, 1952.

3. In the field of Christianity-and-Psychotherapy:

R. Bonthius, *Christian Paths to Self-Acceptance,* Kings Crown, New York, 1948.

Seward Hiltner, *The Christian Shepherd,* Abingdon, New York, 1959.

Seward Hiltner, *Pastoral Counseling,* Abingdon-Cokesbury, New York, 1949.

Rollo May, *Existence* ed. with Ernest Angel and Henri F. Ellenberger, Basic Books, Inc., New York, 1958.

Wayne Oates, *The Religious Dimensions of Personality,* Association Press, New York, 1957.

Wayne Oates, *Religious Factors in Mental Illness,* Association Press, New York, 1955.

Lewis J. Sherrill, *Guilt and Redemption,* John Knox Press, Richmond, Virginia, 1958.

Charles R. Stinnette, *Faith, Freedom and Selfhood,* Seabury, Greenwich, 1959.

Paul Tournier, *The Meaning of Persons,* Harper's, New York, 1957.
Carroll Wise, *Pastoral Counseling,* Harper's, New York, 1951.

Index

Neurosis. See also "conflict," 9, Ch. II (9–32), Ch. III (33–55), 77, 100, 104, 110; and religion, 31f., Chs. VI–VIII.
New Testament, The, 142f., 149.
Niebuhr, Reinhold, 86.
Nietzsche, Friedrich, 79, 127.
Non-directive counseling. See also "permissiveness," 44.

Objectivity, 42, 57, 59, 61n., 147.
Original righteousness, 86.
Original sin. See "sin."
Oxford Group movement, 54.

Parental domination, 16ff., 61ff., 100f.
Pascal, Blaise, 79.
Pastoral counseling, xiv, 3, 49.
Paul, St., 95, 104.
Pelagius, 95f.
Penal system, The, 73.
Perfectionism, 81, 124, 126f., 131, 139.
Permissiveness, 37ff., 41f.
Philosophy, xiii, 73, 75, 79, 83, 86f., 90, 94, 151.
Plato, 87, 88n., 133.
Pope, The, 68.
Pragmatism, 79.
Pratt, J. B., 146.
Predestination, 104, 121f.
Private judgment, 66f., 84.
Problem of evil, The, 113, 122.
Progress, 8, 103, 150.
Projection, 25, 42, 116, 144.
Prometheus, 91.
Protestantism, xiv, xvi, 62, 67f., 83, 85, 139, 149–51.
Psychologism, 144–48, 153.

Psychology of religion, The, xiv, 145–48.
Psycho-pathic personality, 99n.
Psychosis, 9, 34, 71f., 93, 109, 127, 132, 138.
Psycho-somatic unity, 41, 88, 93, 98, 106, 131, 133, 136.
Psychotherapist (role of), 34ff., 52, 113f., 116.
Punishment. See also "divine judgment," 54, 129f., 139.
Purgation, 49.

Rationalism, 86f., 134, 144.
Rationalization, 12, 42, 52, 72.
Reason, and emotion, 59, 72, 92, 97; and faith, 73–84.
Rebellion, 17, 61–3, 72, 97, 101, 128.
Redemption, 69, 83, 96, 108f., 111, 119f., 123, 125, 127, 132, 135, 138, 141, 143, 148, 150–52.
Religion (nature of), 57f., 60, 63f., 65f., 73, 83f., 86f., 144–47.
Religious training, 62ff.
Repression, 12f., 30, 84, 137.
Resistance, 39, 48, 50–52, 54f., 68, 97.
Responsibility. See also "freedom," 11, 18, 29, 40, 82f., Ch. VI (94–103), VII (104–17), 120, 139.
Revelation, 77f., 83, 119, 134, 149, 151–53.
Roman Catholicism, 62, 68, 85, 149.
Rosicrucianism, 54.
Rousseau, Jean-Jacques, 105.
Russell, Bertrand, 128n.

Sacraments, 70f., 124.
Salvation. See also "beatitude,"
"redemption," and "whole-
ness," 107–9, Ch. VIII (118–
28), Ch. IX (129–43), 148.
Schopenhauer, Arthur, 79.
Science, 40, 57, 59, 72f., 78, 86–
8, 90, 103, 105f., 114f., 121,
145, 147–51.
Secularism, 70, 74, 83f., 92f.,
103, 131, 151f.
Security, 18, 30, 57f., 70, 77, 80,
86, 102, 109f., 116f., 134.
Self. See "*ego*," "freedom," "hu-
man nature," "integration,"
and "wholeness."
Self-analysis, 37.
Self-hatred, 109, 127, 139.
Self-love, 53, 128, 129, 134, 138.
Self-sacrifice, 123, 128, 135, 137–
40.
Self-sufficiency, 86, 108, 114, 116.
Sex, 20ff., 63, 91, 136f.
Sin (including "original sin"),
85ff., 91, 95ff., Ch. VII (104–
17), 118–20, 123–26, 148,
151–53.
Skepticism. See also "doubt,"
71f., 81, 144.
Social conditioning. See also
"cultural patterns," 96, 100f.,
104f., 109, 115, 145, 153.
Socrates, 105.
Spengler, Oswald, 87.
Spinoza, Baruch, 79.

Stimulus-response, 41.
Suffering, 135, 139–41.
Super-ego, The. See also "con-
science," "moral standards,"
23f., 110.
Supernatural, The, 75.
Suppression, 13, 110.
Symbolism, 53, 86f., 89.

Telepathy, 44.
Theism, 76, 87, 147, 151.
Theology. See also "doctrine,"
83, 94, 114, 118ff., 126, 144,
148–54.
Theology of Crisis, The, 83,
126f., 128n., 132, 133n., 148–
53.
Tiebout, Harry, 79n.
Total depravity, 85.
Toynbee, Arnold, 87.
Tradition (religious), 62, 66–8,
73, 88.
Transference, 45, 54.

Unamuno, Miguel de, 16.

Value-judgments, 57, 74, 77, 89,
118, 147.
Verbalization, 54f.

"We-feeling," 102.
Wholeness. See also "integration" and "salvation," 41, 53,
76, 132f., 136f.